become
a
~~good~~
GREAT
artist

kristy gordon

become a ~~good~~ GREAT artist

Gain Confidence in Your Art, Find Your Creative Voice and Launch a Thriving Career

PAGE STREET
PUBLISHING CO.

PAGE STREET
PUBLISHING CO.

First published in 2024 by

Page Street Publishing Co.

27 Congress Street, Suite 1511

Salem, MA 01970

www.pagestreetpublishing.com

Distributed by Macmillan, sales in Canada by The Canadian Manda Group.

28   27   26   25   24   1   2   3   4   5

ISBN-13: 979-889003-042-9

Library of Congress Control Number: 2023949793

Edited by Franny Donington-Ayad

Cover and book design by Laura Benton for Page Street Publishing Co.

For the full list of contributing artists, please see page 173.

Printed and bound in China

dedication

I dedicate this book to everyone who follows their excitement as they create. The great art spirit is moving through all of us and expressing itself in different ways. We are all part of the great web of life, and I am grateful to be on this creative journey with you.

contents

Jan 4, 2005

Kristy Gordon
Comic Journal

preface:
my story

I was a talented, hardworking artist who was transfixed by the experience of watching an image emerge on the canvas. My biggest desire was to feel as though I had "made it" as an artist. I wanted to have a clear and recognizable artistic voice so that I could show my work in galleries and have people recognize my work as mine. I also wanted to make a living doing it. And I did everything I could to make this happen.

I studied in academies and ateliers, apprenticed under artists I admired, got a BFA and an MFA and even moved to New York City, all to pave the way to success as an artist. And yet, I couldn't seem to find my artistic voice.

The idea of making it as an artist was put in my head when I was around 9 years old. I remember being in the garden and excitedly telling my mom that I knew what I wanted to be when I grew up—an artist! Mom immediately told me, "That isn't a good career option."

"What do you mean? I can't be an artist?" I cried. "You always tell me that I can be anything I want to be!"

Kristy Gordon
Girl with Tutu

She said, "There are a lot of good artists in the world but very few artists *make it*—living in New York City and showing in galleries, making a lot of money. It's almost impossible."

Despite her unsupportive career advice, Mom did encourage me and my sister, Jessica Gordon, to make art. My mom was an aspiring artist herself, and she taught me how to stretch canvas when I was 16. I remember feeling artistically free and in the flow as a teenager. I was painting unique and colorful paintings that easily flowed out of me, such as the painting *Girl with Tutu*.

Bev Gordon (top left)
Sentinel

Jessica Gordon (bottom left)
Ontario Forest

Philip Craig (top right)
Lily Pads on a Pond During Sunrise

Shannon Craig (bottom right)
Approaching Rain

Still, when it was time to pick a career after high school, I decided to go into animation because it seemed like a good compromise: an artistic path where I could still make a "decent" living.

I got my first job in animation in 1999, where I learned solid drawing and anatomy skills (something often left out of the curriculum of art colleges today) and also how to depict movement. Although animation ultimately wasn't where my heart was, each piece of my path contributed in a meaningful way to my artistic voice. And the universe has a way of magically putting us back on the path we're supposed to be on, even if we take a little detour for a while.

My life changed forever in 2000, when I met Philip Craig, a successful oil painter and the owner of the animation company I was working for. Phil painted large, luscious landscapes in a style that was immediately recognizable. He was always traveling for solo shows in different cities, and he also made a lot of money! I couldn't believe it. I had been lied to. I was told this was impossible. Yet here he was, a full-blown successful artist! *If he could do it, I could do it*, I thought.

Right around the time I met Phil, his daughter, Shannon Craig, who was my age, was also embarking on a career as a full-time painter. This sealed the deal. Clearly it really was possible to be an artist after all!

I started taking painting classes with Phil in 2001, and through him I connected to my first art gallery. I was overjoyed, hyper and elated when the gallery started exhibiting my landscape paintings and actually selling them. My life was complete. The comic at the beginning of this book is a page from my comic journal a year and a half later (2005), showing how my life had changed. I had left my animation job, and I was doing the impossible. Painting for galleries was now my career.

As time wore on, I began to aspire to more. I didn't just want to make a living as an artist, I wanted to *make it* as an artist. I'd lie in the bath reading art magazines and dreaming of the life I'd like to have. I imagined showing in national galleries and being featured in magazines.

There was a series of articles in *International Artist* magazine called "The Academy Way" by an artist named Juan Martínez. The articles showed how to draw and paint using an academic approach that was so realistic it was like looking at a Renaissance painting! I figured, *If I could paint like that, I could paint anything*, and in 2006, I registered for Juan's next workshop. With shaky legs I showed up to Juan's workshop and was blown away that in one single workshop my work was transformed forever. I could now paint people who looked almost hyperreal, inspiring me to switch from landscape painting to figure painting.

However, that created a dilemma for my gallery. It's very difficult to switch your style once you're showing with a gallery, and because I was making a shift, I had to discuss it with my beloved first art gallery director. As kind as he was, he didn't think he had a market for my new work. In 2007, we ended on very good terms, but I was so sad to close that precious chapter of my life.

Although the shift to academically trained art enhanced my technical skills, it also imposed a rigid paradigm that stifled my artistic freedom. I started to feel the inner call to explore what my artistic voice would actually look like. Every painting I created looked different, and most seemed to be too heavily inspired by the work of another artist. I wanted to have a distinct style that was unique to me.

My struggle intensified when I received scathing feedback from a prestigious gallery in Toronto. I was thrilled when the gallery agreed to include my paintings in a few of their group shows, but each time I spoke with the gallery director, she would lecture me about what it was to be a "real artist." The gallerist would explain that I needed to have a "style" and a "message." I looked at the abstract landscapes that she was showing in her gallery and asked what their message was. She couldn't explain it but firmly said I needed to have a message.

I felt so dejected. Here I was showing in the gallery of my dreams, but the gallery director didn't respect me or my work. Reeling from the criticism, I enrolled in an accredited fine arts college in search of my elusive artistic identity.

Juan Martínez (top left)
Hummingbirds

Kristy Gordon (top right)
Woman in Dress

Kristy Gordon (bottom)
Garibaldi Trail

Despite my efforts at experimentation at Ontario College of Art and Design (OCAD), I still couldn't seem to find my voice. To my pain and exasperation, my work still felt overly influenced by whichever artist I admired. I felt like I was the only one who couldn't find my voice. By the end of OCAD, my productivity had gone way down. I now felt not good enough technically and also bad at experimenting.

Still running from the deep feeling of being undereducated and the pain of being told I wasn't a "real Artist" (with a capital A), I enrolled in an MFA in painting at New York Academy of Art in 2011. Continuing my pattern of compare and despair, I *compared* myself to all the other students and despaired that I was, indeed, a failure.

I came out of my MFA having invested everything I had in that experience— my time, my money and my whole life—and still hadn't found my artistic voice. The training was top-notch, and I saw many of my fellow students go through the program, find their voice and even rise to art fame. However, my attachment to creating "good" art and my inability to tap into my own artistic impulses brought me to a point of extreme depression and frustration. It became harder and harder to paint at all. I hated everything I painted and felt more blocked than ever.

Kristy Gordon (top)
Rise

Kristy Gordon (bottom)
Passing Through II

I was listening to Napoleon Hill's book *Think and Grow Rich* during this tumultuous period, and one of the things he advised was to devote yourself entirely to your cause—to burn the bridge behind you. This would leave you no backup plan. You would succeed or die.

As I sat there in my Brooklyn apartment, I realized that this was exactly where I found myself. I was good at art and nothing else. I now lived in New York City, had huge rent bills to pay and was in SO much debt. I *had* to figure this out. There was no other option.

That day would change the entire course of my artistic life. In fact, I truly believe that some higher force, or God (call it what you will), took pity on me that day.

I had been reading Stuart Wilde's book *Miracles*, which sets out a systematic approach to creating miracles in life. *I need a miracle here*, I thought.

Miracles described how to devise a systematic plan of action to create the miracle I craved. Sometimes the miracle would come about because of these actions and sometimes it would come by some other means, but by taking these daily actions, I'd be creating an opening for the miracle to come.

On September 12, 2015, I somberly made a list of daily actions consisting of everything I could think of that could lead me to find my unique artistic expression. I stuck it on the wall beside my bed. Intuitively, I *knew* these actions would bring the result I so desperately longed for: to find my artistic voice.

MY MIRACLE ACTION PLAN

- ❑ **Paint for 25 minutes a day.**

- ❑ **Do one thumbnail (a loose sketch for a painting) a day.**

- ❑ **Do one intuitive painting (painting the first thing that comes to your mind and entirely letting go of making it look good) a day.**

- ❑ **Read one artist interview or article a day.**

- ❑ **Read about color theory or composition daily.**

I looked at my list. I could have kissed it. (I probably did.) Intuitively, I knew that these simple steps would change my life. I committed myself to each of these actions every day and did it as a 21-day challenge. I chose an accountability partner, the amazing artist Gaetanne Lavoie, whom I committed to texting every day to confirm I had done my daily miracle actions.

Kristy Gordon (top)
Journey of Dreams **installation at LIC Arts Open, NYC**

Gaetanne Lavoie (bottom)
The Double Plus One

I started to paint every day for at least 25 minutes, and what I found was that the more I painted, the more inspiration flowed. And because it was focused work, I got more done than I usually did in hours. I didn't spend time pushing paint around with no idea what I was doing. Often, I would feel like I was ruining a painting for the entire session, but frequently I'd sit back at the end and realize that in fact I'd made it slightly better. Occasionally, I truly had made it worse, but at least I knew that direction didn't work, so it was still useful.

I began to develop a faith in the process. I no longer felt like I had to have it all figured out to get started. I saw that ideas came to me as I painted. More ideas started to flow simply because I was more consistent with my painting time.

The process was life-altering. Even though I didn't feel like I was painting that much (25 minutes a day is a very sustainable pace), I was getting more done than I had in years!

Kristy Gordon in studio (top)

Before the 21-day challenge, I had started so many paintings, but nothing was getting finished. During and after the challenge, I gradually finished all of them, and to my shock and amazement, I was happy with them! It was so satisfying to realize that if I just paint something—anything—for 25 minutes every day, slowly but surely, everything will get finished! After the 21-day challenge was over, I had developed new habits that I carried forward.

With this new series of completed paintings that felt authentic to me, I had a solo show fall into my lap. It felt very vulnerable to show this new body of paintings to the world, but it was also extremely exciting because it was my first solo show in New York City!

EIGHT YEARS LATER

Since that pivotal day in 2015, I've loosely kept up with the basic daily structure of my Miracle Action Plan. To my surprise and relief, I did find my voice as an artist. That first solo show in New York consisted of the work I'd done during the 21-day challenge that marked the beginning of feeling like I was truly creating authentic work. What I discovered is that all my work, through all the phases of my life, had always had elements of my voice in it, but after the challenge, everything seemed to come together in a

cohesive body that felt uniquely "me." Since then, my work has evolved as I evolve as a person, but each painting has felt authentic and has contained similar threads, like exploring magic, mystery and the future for humanity.

It's surprising that my galleries actually stuck with me through this shift to authentic work. But they loved my new work so much that we organized solo and group shows around my new series. I had numerous magazine articles feature the new paintings, and I even wrote a couple of articles in magazines about how to find your voice as an artist!

I also grew large Instagram and TikTok followings (@kristygordonart on both). My work won prizes, and as I mentioned, I had my first solo exhibition in New York City. That was particularly meaningful because of my mom's words when I was a child: "Very

Kristy Gordon
Planetary **installation at Langham Cultural Centre, Kaslo, BC**

few artists make it—living in New York City and showing in galleries . . ."

The 13-step framework that I've developed for connecting with our artistic voice consists of clearing blocks, creating a habit, working intuitively, brainstorming with thumbnails and knowing your world.

Whatever your art goals are, whether it's to connect with your true self, show in galleries, win prizes, make a lot of money, be featured in magazines or have a large following on social media, these things can all fall into place when you find your artistic voice.

While I can't guarantee artistic fame and fortune, by following these steps, I can guarantee a deeply fulfilling artistic practice and the satisfaction of knowing yourself in your art.

THIS COURSE

There is a huge difference between wanting to be a great artist and showing up regularly to your practice. This course will serve as a compass steering you toward becoming the artist you are meant to be. It begins by helping you set a clear intention to make meaningful, authentic art, and then it guides you through practical steps in 13 weekly lessons to transform your vision into a reality.

These lessons provide actionable insights on clarifying your artistic vision, releasing creative blocks, tapping into your intuition, brainstorming ideas and refining your craft. I've had the honor of assisting countless artists through these transformative steps, saving them the years of struggle and failure that I had to go through. While I can't guarantee overnight fame, I promise that by undertaking this course, you will tap into your own artistic inclinations, and by allowing authenticity to guide your work, you will become magnetic to the career success that you desire.

There is a chapter for each week with a lesson aimed at a specific stage of this process followed by an activity to help you turn each step into an action. As long as you do each assignment—however imperfectly—you will get the results: a free and flowing creative practice that is authentic and deeply satisfying. Creativity is our natural state, and it is waiting for you.

To do this course, you will need to set aside one hour a day. The crux of the program is the 25 minutes of creative work as well as the daily brain-drain writing. You may want to grab an accountability partner and work through this course together to discuss your weekly progress. The 13 weekly lessons will give you tools that will guide you to artistic freedom and confidence in your artistic voice.

COURSE SUPPLY LIST

In addition to your regular art supplies, here are the materials you'll need for this course:

- ❑ Journal
- ❑ Roll of white craft paper
- ❑ Kids' acrylic paints
- ❑ Paintbrushes
- ❑ Vision board (I like a large piece of foam core board.)

- ❑ Sketchbook
- ❑ Felt pens
- ❑ Pencil crayons (optional)
- ❑ Black permanent marker (I use Sharpie®.)
- ❑ Colored plasticine

week

identifying
the components
of your voice

1

This week we are going to explore what our artistic voice is, what it will look like stylistically and where it comes from for each of us. When we know our artistic voice, we create truer art. The first step to becoming a great artist is getting in tune with this.

"The one thing you have that nobody else has is you, your voice, your mind, your story, your vision; so, write, and draw, and build, and play, and dance, and live as only you can."

—Neil Gaiman

Fish can't see the water they swim in. Our preferences and stylistic choices in art are like the water we swim in. It can be hard for us to know our true nature because we are so immersed in it. By doing this assignment, you will uncover clues that reveal your own vibration and bring forth your artistic voice.

There is something unique and special inside all of us—something that no one else can offer the world. Our job is not to judge this gift, but to explore it and share it with the world.

Our artistic voice comes from the specific choices we make as artists. These choices give our work an individual style. And when we allow our inner direction to guide our work, we find our artistic voice. But first, we must give ourselves permission by learning to listen to the still, small voice of our intuition nudging us in a certain direction as we work and commit to trying out its ideas.

When we know our voice, we know ourselves. Our voice is reliable and will guide us through the artistic decisions we're faced with as we create. The assignments in this book are going to guide you on a journey of knowing yourself so you can trust your own instincts and have a clear compass to always point you toward your true artistic voice.

There are two main components to the visual language of our voice: style and concept. Artistic style includes elements such as color, line, composition and type of mark-making. Concept refers to the message behind the work.

"To create one's own world in any of the arts takes courage."

—Georgia O'Keeffe

Enrique Martínez Celaya (top, from left)

The Same Places, 2023. Oil and wax on canvas, 92 x 86 inches.

The Words, 2023. Oil and wax on canvas, 92 x 86 inches. Courtesy of the artist.

Photo credit: Heather Rasmussen

Jason Yarmosky (bottom)
Sleep Walking

"What moves men of genius, or rather what inspires their work, is not new ideas, but their obsession with the idea that what has already been said is still not enough."

–Eugène Delacroix

Hieronymus Bosch
The Garden of Earthly Delights,
© Photographic Archive Museo
Nacional del Prado

Jan van Eyck
The Crucifixion; The Last Judgment

The easiest way to get in touch with your artistic preferences is to see what you like in art. So the assignment this week is to compile ten images of your favorite works of art, print them and analyze them, noting key stylistic components. Because I'm a painter, I paid attention to elements such as color, type of mark-making and texture. You will also note any recurring themes and concepts that stand out to you and how they might relate to your background or personal experience. By getting in touch with your personal artistic inclinations and making a list of your preferences, you will have a road map to the key components of your voice.

After doing this assignment, one of the artists in my online art program I teach discovered that she was ignoring her own artistic preferences in her work and simply painting the way her teacher painted, which was super tight. She says she felt as if someone was looking over her shoulder as she worked. This is so common for us as artists. Getting clear about what we like in art gives us the impetus to try it out in our own work.

When I asked Enrique Martínez Celaya, one of my favorite painters, how to find one's artistic voice, he said, "Make a lot of work. Look at a lot of art in galleries and then paint a lot." Otherwise, he said, we can end up getting too theoretical. Gaining inspiration from other artists is not copying. We work out how to integrate the inspiration into our own voice by making a lot of work.

It's important to note the distinction between gaining inspiration and imitating so much you can't tap into your unique voice. It's essential to strike a balance between external influence and personal expression. When I'm borrowing too much from another artist, I'm almost entirely using their language—the same colors, brush techniques and themes. In contrast, when I gain inspiration, I'm often combining multiple sources and integrating these into my own voice.

Some artists go through a phase where it's beneficial to take breaks from the influx of images to focus on their own artistic inclinations and inner impulses. I gained this insight from a conversation I had with artist Jason Yarmosky about how overwhelming and confusing it can be to be so inundated with art images, particularly with social media. I found it helpful to step away from social media for a while and only engage with specific works of art, but some people find they need to put all external images of others' art away for a time in order to tap into their own artistic inclinations.

Currently, my creativity is fed by looking at art, but each person is different, and each person may go through different phases. You will know what you need most by learning to listen to your inner voice and intuition.

Carolyn Janssen
~*(G.O.E.D.)*~, 2014–2015, archival inkjet print, 60 x 103½ inches (152.4 x 262.9 cm)
North Carolina Museum of Art, Raleigh. Commissioned with funds from the William R. Roberson Jr. and Frances M. Roberson Endowed Fund for North Carolina Art, 2014.5/a—c

"Those who do not want to imitate anything,
produce nothing."

—Salvador Dalí

Kristy Gordon
Planetary

assignment

Your first assignment is to collect ten high-resolution images of your favorite works of art—by ten different artists—and print them out as large as possible, in full color (I prefer 11 x 17 inches [28 x 43 cm]). Arrange these printed images next to your art so you can see them beside your own work.

Take out your journal or sketchbook and analyze these works, making note of the following (if they apply to your medium):

❑ **What colors resonate with you the most? Write down three to four colors that recur in at least a few of these images.**

❑ **What shapes or edges are you drawn to? Are they soft edges/hard edges, rounded shapes/pointy shapes or some kind of combination?**

❑ **Is the use of line evident?**

❑ **What compositions do you enjoy (e.g., symmetrical/asymmetrical, simple/ complex, etc.)?**

❑ **What formats stand out? What shapes of canvas or surfaces excite you (or the equivalent in your medium)?**

❑ **What type of mark-making, textural components or paint application do you enjoy? (For example, as a painter, I enjoy transparent passages contrasted with impasto notes. I know a sculptor who enjoys the contrast of industrial metal with soft shapes made from plaster.)**

❑ **Are there any recurring motifs that stand out?**

❑ **What is the subject matter?**

❑ **Do any of these recurring themes and motifs resonate with your cultural background?**

❑ **Does your personal experience influence any of these preferences?**

❑ **In comparing your work to your favorite artworks, is there anything that you enjoy in art that your own work is missing? Write a list of exactly what you like in the works you chose that you don't see in your own work.**

After teaching this program to artists around the world, I discovered it's best not to narrow down your subject matter at this point. Instead, focus on the stylistic components that you enjoy and the types of subject matter that interest you, ideally incorporating a range of subject matter. You will gain more clarity about exactly what you want to create throughout this course, but arbitrarily narrowing it down to one thing at the beginning could block the natural evolution of your voice. Your voice may be broader than you initially think, while still having recurring elements that make it distinctly yours.

Formulate this into a checklist of elements to incorporate into your future work. You now have the main components of your voice!

WHAT YOU WILL GAIN FROM THIS

This exercise acts as a guide for when you feel lost. Sometimes we don't know where to start, and remembering what inspires us can help get the momentum going and assist with problem-solving when you have decisions to make during the creation process. I printed out my list and put it next to my easel. I noted that I liked animal motifs, triptych formats and mystical imagery, and as you can see, they clearly show up in my work.

Your voice will evolve as your interests change over time. My goal isn't to create a painting exactly like any of my favorite artists do, but to see what it is that I enjoy in their work and to intentionally bring that into my own work.

Next week, we'll take a look at your creative process. We'll explore how the imagination works and how you can feed your creativity so that inspiration flows.

"Right now, a moment of time is fleeting by! Capture its reality in paint! To do that we must put all else out of our minds. We must become that moment, make ourselves a sensitive recording plate . . . Give the image of what we actually see, forgetting everything that has been seen before our time."

—Paul Cézanne

week

honing your
creative process
in 25 minutes
a day

2

To find our artistic voice, we need to be immersed in the flow of our creative practice. The nature of what inspires us will be different for everyone, and it's these personal threads of interest that shape our distinctive voice. A consistent art practice is the key to tapping into inspiration and finding our authentic voice.

"Artists, if you're waiting for inspiration to begin something, it won't come. Inspiration only comes from working."
—Jerry Saltz, *New York Magazine* senior art critic

This week we'll explore the workings of your creative process. There are some aspects of creativity that creators almost universally agree on, while there are other ways in which the creative process is different for everyone.

One common consensus is that creative epiphanies and inspiration come when we consistently engage in the process. These moments of insight may come while we're working or even when we're taking a break, like on a walk or in the shower, but regular participation in our creative practice seems to energetically pose the questions that these epiphanies answer.

Many of us think that we must wait for inspiration to strike us like a lightning bolt before we can begin, but one of the most important things we can do for our creative practice is to nurture it daily.

A lot of us live busy lives, and there's no way we can paint 8 hours a day. Attempting to do so will burn us out, or we'll start to ruin a piece toward the end of such a long session. However, I discovered a game changer that transformed my creative practice: painting for 25 minutes a day, no matter what. So this week we'll be using this framework, and we'll explore different contexts to see what works best for your creative process.

I used to create only when I felt inspired, but I found this led to low productivity. I was blocked and never really felt inspired, so I never worked. Meanwhile, I noticed other artists who had started out with less initial skill than me but worked consistently and improved so much that they were surpassing me! They were creating ambitious bodies of new work because they were painting consistently.

It was around that time that I discovered Michael Mackintosh, a "spiritual entrepreneur" whom I stumbled across on YouTube. He changed my life by suggesting dedicating a mere 25 minutes every day to our projects and anchoring this new habit with a 21-day challenge.

Kristy Gordon
Painting in studio

"Inspiration exists,
but it has to find
you working."

–Pablo Picasso

I began painting 25 minutes a day, and that's it. I could barely stomach it at first. I found that during some of the sessions, the 25 minutes were absolutely excruciating, and I felt like I was ruining the painting the entire time. However, it's a short enough span for this torture, so I could tolerate the pain. I discovered that even on a very complex painting there would always be at least one area where I knew what to do for 25 minutes. That became my strategy: Choose whatever it was that I knew what to do on the painting, and paint for 25 minutes no matter what. I set a timer.

I soon started noticing a pattern. Despite feeling like I was messing it up the entire time, stepping back at the end of the session revealed subtle improvements in the painting. Some of the time I had ruined parts, but in hindsight it was an essential part of the process. By attempting to work on those areas, I had identified problems and could fix them. This was profoundly useful in paintings such as *Magick*, where I was attempting to do something new, such as blending the main painting's window-like effect with the painted sculptural effects below.

Kristy Gordon
Magick

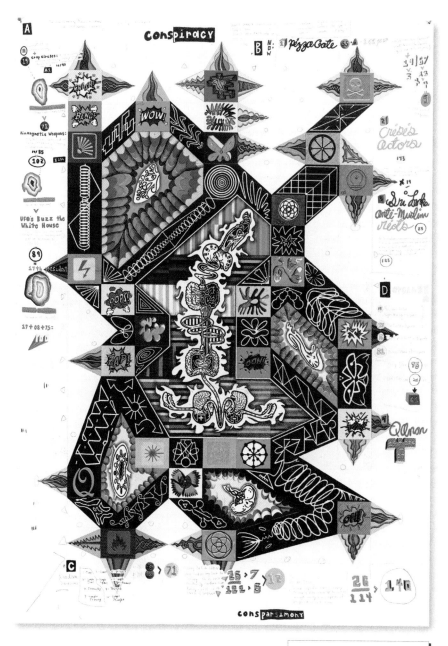

John O'Connor
Conspiracy: Faker Sent INN

I started teaching this framework to fellow artists, emphasizing that we can't control the outcome of anything; we can only control our actions. We can sit down and paint 25 minutes a day, but we can't guarantee that at the end we will be happy with the progress. We may have even made it worse at times, but we will always still benefit from having done it. We will be honing our skills and discovering more of what we want the painting to be, so putting in the time always pays off.

With only 25 minutes, it's focused work—I'm not just pushing paint around. This approach allows epiphanies to enter, as artist John O'Connor described in an interview I did with him on my podcast, *Down2Art*. John highlighted the importance of time in his work, saying that working on a piece for an extended period of time allows layers of inspiration and ideas to enter. Like John, even when I don't know the entire path to complete a painting, I always know the next step. That's what is so exciting about the creative process. Over time, I've developed a trust in the process, knowing that as long as I keep moving forward, the answer will eventually come to me.

John also said he keeps the idea in mind for a work in progress and it becomes like a conversation with the idea. Many artists share this notion. They find that their art takes on a life of its own, guiding the direction of the work. It becomes a process where the artist responds to the changes and revelations the art presents. As the artist stays involved, the art is revealing itself to us!

It's essential that we let go of rigid expectations about making "good art" or sticking too much to an initial vision. The key to a thriving creative practice is to engage with the process of creation daily and stay open to epiphanies as they come. I'm not working in a state of inspiration all the time, and if I required that, I would never get anything done. Instead, by working consistently for 25 minutes a day, we create opportunities for the sparks of inspiration to enter.

Often, once I just get started, I'll paint for more than 25 minutes, but I don't expect that. As long as I do 25 minutes, my job is done. Also, if I paint for more than the allotted time one day, it doesn't count toward the next day. I have to do a minimum of 25 minutes of painting every single day. This is helpful when I'm working on a painting that is breaking new ground for me, as I was with *Uniforms and Ladders*. I had a vague idea that I wanted to subtly embed the idea of an upper world, lower world and middle world into it. By working for 25 minutes a day, I allowed time for the ideas to percolate until slowly I figured out how to do it, and I completed the painting.

Kristy Gordon
Uniforms and Ladders

Daniel Maidman
Natasha

Elizabeth Gilbert's concept of creativity is that there is a little genius who lives outside of ourselves. It's actually an idea inspired by the way the ancient Greeks and Romans conceived of creativity, and it really resonates with me. Our job is to show up and do the work while the creative genius makes it excellent.

Elizabeth says that it's as though ideas are out there just floating around waiting for someone to pick them up and run with them. I once experienced a situation where I had an idea for a painting that I started but didn't finish. Surprisingly, months later, I came across an article in a magazine about another artist and how he developed a particular painting, and it eerily resembled my initial idea. He had definitely never seen my painting, but his had almost the same people with some of the EXACT same poses! It was as if he had picked up the idea from the creative genius and brought it to fruition while I had let it slip away. This taught me that if I have an idea, I should stick with it all the way through to the end, or someone else might!

Artist and art writer Daniel Maidman explains, "There are two ways to see a great project: from above, as a complete shape, and from ground level, inside the maze. You must see the project from both perspectives. It is important to remember why you began and where you hope to go. But it is also important to walk the maze, making a tiny bit of progress every single day. It is that consistent dedication to putting in the work which crosses vast expanses in the end. . . ."

If you've been feeling stuck on one piece or feeling a lack of inspiration for creating in general, this simple practice will help you invite creativity and inspiration in daily.

"You can't wait for inspiration.
You have to go after it with a club."

—Jack London

assignment

Your assignment this week is to uncover what brings the most creative flow to your practice by committing to 25 minutes of creative work a day. And within that framework, experiment with different contexts, such as time of day, for this daily practice. Then journal about what each context brings up. Write down what you will do for yourself when you accomplish this goal. How will you celebrate? For me I took myself and a friend out to dinner to celebrate.

❑   **Each day this week set aside 25 minutes to create, but do it in a variety of contexts.**

❑   **One day, do it in the morning, the next at night and then add on to it from there.**

❑   **Experiment with working in the morning after a long walk.**

❑   **Try creating in the evening after a hot bath.**

❑   **Create after looking at all your favorite art books and spreading them out on the floor open to your favorite images.**

❑   **Make your art with the images you printed out during Week 1 taped to the wall around your easel so you can see them as you work.**

❑   **Try creating when you've put all images by other artists away.**

❑   **Do something to create a ritual around your creative practice. It could be burning incense, lighting a candle, setting up your space in a specific way, playing music or whatever works for you.**

❑   **See if it's motivating to give yourself a treat at the end of your 25 minutes.**

❑   **Create a sketch in 3 minutes, and then use it to create a full-scale work of art, even if you have no idea how to do it. Trust that you will fill in the blanks later. Perhaps have your favorite art surrounding you as you start so you can gain inspiration for colors (if you work with color). Start by boldly mapping out the large shapes working from your sketch.**

❑   **Write down what worked best for you and why.**

❑   **Journal about times you were most creative and in the flow as well about times when you were blocked. Jot down anything you remember doing or thinking in both phases. Make a list of what works for you and what doesn't.**

WHAT YOU WILL GAIN FROM THIS

This exercise will help you clarify how to get into the flow and plant the seeds for inspiration in your creative practice. It will also help you start the habit of spending 25 minutes a day in the process of creation.

This will nurture your creativity and allow the magic to enter your practice, so that you will experience joy and excitement about creating every day. The more fulfilled you feel by your creative practice, the more you will want to create, which will allow even more ideas and inspiration to flow to you!

Next week, we'll look at how to tackle any fears related to your art.

"Don't think about making art, just get it done. Let everyone else decide if it's good or bad, whether they love it or hate it. While they're deciding, make even more art."

—Andy Warhol

week

overcoming your limiting beliefs

3

Many of us have been running from our artistic blocks and limiting beliefs for a very long time. We've shoved down disappointment, downplayed the impact of criticism and convinced ourselves that we were staying ahead of the pain. Meanwhile, we have no idea why it is getting harder and harder to show up for our creative practice.

"Fears about artmaking fall into two families: fears about yourself and fears about your reception by others."

—David Bayles, author of *Art & Fear*

This week we'll be inventorying both categories of fear: fear about ourselves and fear about our reception from others. Then we'll work on overcoming them. Artistic flow comes when we face our feelings, even though everything in us tells us otherwise. We think that if we look at the pain of our self-doubt, we'll be convinced our fears are right. Strangely enough, however, it's the other way around. Our fears only persist until we face our insecurities. That's why as the years passed, I was getting more blocked and feeling worse about myself artistically.

Unfortunately, it's very common for us artists to receive criticism. Often the people closest to us say something offhandedly that they barely think about, but as sensitive artists, their comments can really hurt us deep down. That's the thing with being an artist—we want this. We want it so badly. If it doesn't work out, we can't say, "Oh well, I don't really care anyway." We do care. We care a lot. That's a good thing, but we must take care of ourselves and process our pain and disappointment. We have to boldly face our feelings and strategize about how to keep moving forward.

I encapsulated this thought in my painting on the next page, which depicts figures struggling in the underworld, balancing positive and negative forces with a nod toward the wonder of the great mystery behind it all.

A lot of my friends had early success, and after completing my MFA and not having the same success, I assumed I was a failure. It was one of my biggest limiting beliefs. But a funny thing happened along the way. A lot of those friends felt trapped in their early work, whereas I had the freedom to explore my voice out of the public eye. And eventually, I made a career out of helping other artists overcome their limiting beliefs, which I would never have been able to do if I had that early-on success.

"The progress of any writer is marked by those moments when he manages to outwit his own inner police system."

—Ted Hughes

Kristy Gordon (top)
A Daily Reprieve

Katherine Bradford (bottom)
Storm at Sea

I felt great relief after reading an interview in the *Brooklyn Rail* with one of my favorite artists, Katherine Bradford, where she said, "[It] takes a long time to develop a very personal vocabulary. It certainly took me years and years to find my own voice. And I wouldn't say it has anything to do with age; it had to do with sticking to it, and doing it a lot, like an athlete."

I had a breakthrough with my artistic fears while reading Julia Cameron's seminal book *The Artist's Way*. In it, she describes "morning pages" as a powerful tool in removing limiting beliefs and blocks. I wasn't sure it would work. (After all, she's a writer and I'm a painter.) But she assured readers that these pages are effective for any discipline. Excited and hopeful, I started right away. Every morning, as soon as I woke up, I wrote out three pages of free-flowing writing. Most of the time these pages were negative, self-pitying and angry.

Julia also suggested journaling on specific instances where readers had felt very hurt artistically. I wrote about a teacher who told me I wasn't experimenting enough right at a point where I felt like I was experimenting more than ever. I also wrote about an experience I'd had where my grandma's boyfriend saw a nude painting of mine and said, "Shame on you." That was the last time I saw him or my grandma, as they both passed on soon after. I had ignored it at the time and felt like I had a tough skin, but beneath the surface, comments like these were weighing very heavily on me. Deep down I was thinking I should be ashamed of myself, that I wasn't a good artist, and I wasn't good at experimenting. I wrote out every detail, expanding on each incident as much as I could. I cried for my younger self inside me who wanted to be a great artist, who wanted to be admired and have people respect her for her art . . . the vulnerable artist who felt so crushed by these inconsiderate comments. I cried a lot. Finally, I was being completely honest with myself.

Then a strange thing happened. I was able to paint again. I didn't feel like a secretly bad and shameful artist anymore. I had separated from that. I knew I was an artist, and I knew it was all I'd ever wanted to be, so now I was determined to get back on track.

Over time, I discovered that writing these morning pages (which I call "brain-drain pages") in the evening also helped me sleep. So now I do them any time of day, and I swear by them to keep me in the flow, prevent me from getting artistically blocked and keep my life as manageable and on track as possible.

"In principle, an art without emotion
is not art."

—Paul Cézanne

By journaling about specific events, I was able to release the fears about how my work was being received by others. To get in touch with the limiting beliefs I had about myself, I followed Julia Cameron's next suggestion, which was to write down an affirmation ten times. I wrote, "I am a dedicated, talented artist creating meaningful work." And then I paid attention to the negative critical responses that immediately occurred to me.

For instance, some thoughts that I got were, *In what world . . . You wish! . . . You're lazy . . . You barely work! . . . You can't do anything right . . . Not likely . . . Dream on! . . . So egotistical . . . You have no voice of your own!*

When choosing an affirmation, you can use the one that I've written here, choose one you've found somewhere else or create one that resonates strongly with you.

"Have no fear of perfection, you'll never reach it."

—Salvador Dalí

Kristy Gordon
Kristy in front of *Strangled Planet*

When you do this in the assignment, you'll likely encounter a condemning thought for every positive affirmation you write. Most of these thoughts will be phrases you've heard before, perhaps things that were said to you as a child. Reflect on times you've heard these harsh statements. This voice in your head is relentless and won't let you do anything without giving its cruel criticism. When I did this exercise, it brought me to tears as I realized a major factor in my artistic block was this deep-seated programming operating beneath my conscious awareness.

This inner judge had me doubting every single brushstroke I made. No wonder it was so hard to paint. My inner critic was literally telling me everything I did was wrong and that I would never amount to anything. It was borderline abusive.

I tried to remember times I had heard these phrases before, but as familiar as they were, I couldn't pinpoint the origin of these thoughts. But bringing them to my conscious awareness gave me deep compassion for myself. Through practice I got better at seeing that these condemnations weren't true. Even if I couldn't immediately recognize a limiting belief as false, this practice put some space between those thoughts and myself, allowing me to at least consider that they weren't true.

The artist Brian Cirmo says, "In my experience as an artist, self-doubt never goes away. To overcome self-doubt in my work I have built an army of artists. These artists, dead and alive, share my sensibilities, my convictions, my concepts and vision." Brian explains, "They justify the work I make; help root it in art history, make it relevant in the contemporary art world and simultaneously protect my work against self-doubt and the naysayers." Brian's painting *Bulb* perfectly portrays what our inner critic is like, constantly lurking in the shadows.

"Your fear will always be triggered by your creativity, because creativity asks you to enter into realms of uncertain outcome, and fear hates uncertain outcome."

–Elizabeth Gilbert

"If you hear a voice within you saying, 'You are not a painter,' then by all means paint and that voice will be silenced."

–Vincent van Gogh

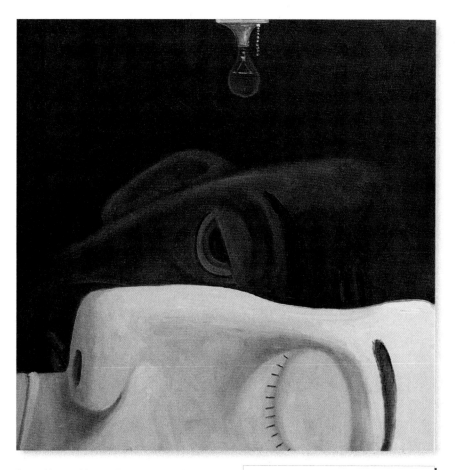

Brian Cirmo
Bulb

Sometimes the voice in our head is very convincing. By dedicating 25 minutes a day to your creative practice, you stay committed to your work long enough to see these harsh judgments aren't true. You started to implement this in the second week of this program. By building on the practice of 25 minutes a day along with this week's exercise, we are beginning the path toward uncovering our artistic voice. We find that we CAN create and complete powerful work; we DO have an artistic voice and we ARE dedicated, talented artists creating meaningful work.

"The main thing is to be moved, to love, to hope, to tremble, to live."

—Auguste Rodin

assignment

The most effective approach I've found for overcoming art-related fears, blocks and limiting beliefs is adapted from Julia Cameron's book *The Artist's Way*. Starting this week, write three pages of free-flowing writing every day. Julia suggests we do this in the morning, which I often do, but you can do them anytime. In fact, sometimes it helps me sleep if I do them just before bed.

I suggest adding these brain-drain writing pages to your life forever. Usually these pages will be completely undirected, with you writing whatever comes to your mind—whether it's your lists of things to do, complaints about your life, everything you're worried about or even everything you're grateful for!

One day this week use the time in a more directed way. Get out your journal and a pen and make time to write out three full pages, each page a rumination on the following three topics (special thanks to *The Artist's Way* for providing the template for this section):

PART 1: REFLECTING ON PAST EXPERIENCE

❑   **Identifying Disappointments: Make a list of art-related disappointments, criticisms or events that left you feeling hurt.**

❑   **Deep Dive: Choose the most significant experience from your list of disappointments and journal about it more deeply. Where were you? Who was involved? What happened? How did you feel? And what did you internalize from the event?**

❑   **Speaking Up: Now, talk back to the offender. Stand up for yourself. Say what you didn't say to the person or entity that you know is true.**

PART 2: INSIGHTS ABOUT YOUR INNER CRITIC

❑   **Positive Statements: Write ten positive statements about yourself, your art or your creative practice, each one sentence long. Each sentence will be different.**

❑   **Inner Critic: Pay attention to any immediate harsh responses you hear in your mind after writing the positive statements and write these criticisms down.**

❑   **Diverse Criticisms: Notice the differing criticisms you receive for each positive statement.**

- ❑ Reflective Analysis: **Reflect on when you've heard these critical statements before.**

- ❑ Journaling: **If you can remember instances associated with the critical statements, write about those situations in detail.**

PART 3: INTEGRATING YOUR INSIGHTS

- ❑ Addressing Avoidance: **Journal on what you're avoiding by not doing some aspect of your creative work. For instance, are you avoiding experimentation, or not finishing projects or just not showing up for your creative practice at all? If so, how are you avoiding finding out that the inner critic is right by not showing up to your creative practice?**

- ❑ Unmasking the Inner Critic: **Recognize that this avoidance is perpetuating the inner critic's narrative. Journal about the phrases that came to you in Part 2, and tie them to your avoidance patterns. For example, within the admonition "You can't do anything right," I was consciously feeling like every brushstroke was a mistake (even though it wasn't). And unconsciously, I started avoiding painting altogether, thus inadvertently proving my inner critic right because I believe that it is "right" for an artist to create work.**

- ❑ Reframing: **Consider your current situation (whatever has happened that's brought you to where you are now). What possible benefit could there be to this phase?**

WHAT YOU WILL GAIN FROM THIS

This exercise will act as a solvent when you're feeling hurt. Without necessarily knowing how it works, you will notice that flow is returning to your creative life and self-doubt is leaving you. Once you start writing, you will swear by these brain-drain pages like I do!

Next week, we'll explore the use of intuitive painting to recover a sense of play in your art.

week

recovering
a sense
of play

4

This week, we will reconnect with our intuition and the innate sense of play in creating. We'll use the powerful practice of intuitive painting to tap into our gut responses and shine light on neglected parts of ourselves while entering into a state of creative flow.

"We are all born creative. Accessing your creative self is as easy as breathing (with a little coaxing). Call back your inner four-year-old and remember the joy and excitement when you were given crayons, rattles, paint, and paper. Remember a time before you had to be good at something, a time before inhibitions."

—Damini Celebre

Many of us have been conditioned to feel that who we are and what we think are wrong. We've learned to question our natural impulses and stuff down our feelings, but to find our artistic voice, we must reconnect with the wholeness of our being.

When I completed my MFA in painting and began teaching, I found myself envious of the beginners in my classes because they embodied a free and playful approach to painting. This was something that I deeply longed for since my approach had become very rigid and logical.

I remembered when I was a kid and creativity flowed effortlessly. Yet as time passed, I developed my technical skills and also accumulated art rejections and criticism and began to lose that sense of wonder.

I discovered intuitive painting from Damini Celebre's book *Painting the Landscape of Your Soul* and immediately got excited because I knew this would transform my art. Intuitive painting is where you listen to your gut impulse and do that—you hear it, don't question it, and do it. Then do your next thought. Intuitive painting bypasses the logical side of your brain and allows your inner child/inner artist to play. You can spend as long as you want on this. Ten minutes is totally sufficient, and sometimes you'll get absorbed in it for much longer. Also if you want, this can count toward your 25 minutes of creation a day. Some days I count it, and other days I don't.

I bought a roll of white craft paper and some children's acrylic paints and committed to doing one intuitive painting a day. I would do them on the floor, which enhanced the kid-like playfulness of the experience.

"I don't say everything, but I paint everything."

—Pablo Picasso

Kristy Gordon
Intuitive painting examples

Kristy Gordon (top)
The Cosmic Lotus

Kristy Gordon (bottom)
The Cosmic Lotus Intuitive Painting

"If I could say it in words there would be no reason to paint."

—Edward Hopper

I did this every day for a few months. Some of my intuitive paintings looked pretty bad, but some looked pretty cool. A couple of them absolutely mesmerized me, and I ended up using them as studies for larger paintings. But that is not the goal. The only goal is to strengthen your connection to your gut impulse.

For instance, my painting *The Cosmic Lotus* was conceived of from an intuitive painting. I liked the image so much that I expanded it to a 5 x 8-foot (1.5 x 2.5-m) painting. It became the main painting in my exhibition called *Planetary* and was featured in a six-page article in *Galleries West* magazine. Later it sold to a major art collector!

In a somatic approach to healing, intuitive painting allows us to access, express and release emotions that have become trapped in the body. Damini Celebre emphasizes that "Our intuitive self knows how to bring these shadow parts into the light and heal them."

One block I had been experiencing was feeling like a fraud—as though I was a copycat and had no real voice of my own. As I tuned into my body and sensed where the tightness was, I located the feeling stored in my belly area, the second chakra, which is the energy center just below the navel and is tied to creativity. I engaged in a dialogue with this stuck energy, asking it how it would like to express itself in color and form. The response I got was, "Start with a gross muddy color—brown mixed with yellow ochre." Initially I was guided to glob it on so it looked as gross as possible. Although thinking, *This painting is going to look horrible*, I obeyed. Next, I was directed to lay a very flat blood-red color on top of the mud. I started liking how the painting was looking, but then a few black drips fell off my brush, landing in the flat red, and I felt like crying. The accidental drips activated my inner perfectionist, which was constantly criticizing everything I did. My inner subconscious mind guided me to do big teardrop shapes over the whole thing. All the paint was wet and thick, and I felt frustration welling up inside me as the white mixed with the wet red. This was not going as planned.

Kristy Gordon
Intuitive painting example

I remembered Damini Celebre's motto about intuitive painting: "Ruin it early and ruin it often." I felt guided to add blue. Even though blue didn't fit with the warm color scheme, I added it anyway. The painting got muddier and muddier. Remembering that with intuitive painting the key is to lean into whatever comes up, I picked up my wet palette and smeared it directly into that mud I had created, and then I mushed it around with my hand. I was proud of myself for embracing the muddiness instead of trying to fix it. The painting was almost complete. I scratched a heart into the mud pile's center with my finger, a symbol of completion and transformation.

After doing the exercise I noticed that I became aware in my studio practice of when I was getting overly attached to making a painting perfect. That was a mindset that was preventing the boldness and painterly approach I admired to come through in my own work. I started to let bold strokes that hadn't been fiddled with endlessly remain on the canvas. I also realized it was really my perfectionism that was the biggest block to having a playful approach, and not that I was a fraud or a copycat.

New York–based artist Lisa Lebofsky says, "Dictating the conversation stifles the magic in painting. The paint is as fluid as our emotions, so I let them run through my body into a mark-making dance often surprising and always exciting. The surface and the mark drive the direction of the painting. I only mediate the interaction of the brush to surface and am along for the ride."

Intuitive painting works for all disciplines and will assist in healing shadow parts as well as bringing flow and authenticity regardless of whether you're a painter or not. This intuitive approach to creating has its roots in the surrealism movement of the early twentieth century. Artists would use forms of automatism to generate ideas for their work, such as using automatic writing or making a random scribble and using chance to reveal repressed aspects within the subconscious.

You could experiment with other forms of automatic creation beyond paint if you'd like. Some sculptors make tiny intuitive sculptures. The New York–based sculptor and installation artist Kelsey Tynik uses a combination of intuitive collage as well as automatic drawing in her practice, and she says they bring intuition and play to her work, often generating ideas for her large-scale sculptures and installations.

Similarly, sculptor Sherlin Hendrick says that when she created her iconic series of sculptures that paired an animal with an emotion, she initiated a self-imposed game of embracing her intuition as her guide. Her rule was simple. If she had a thought, she had to follow it. She says that *Anxiety Rabbit* popped up first, and it went from there, leading to a surprising series of creative revelations. She didn't know where it would go, but she just kept following her intuitive impulses until the entire show had been created.

"Painting is easy when you don't know how, but very difficult when you do."

–Edgar Degas

Lisa Lebofsky (top)
Ilulissat Glacier

Kelsey Tynik (bottom left)
Sometimes human places, create inhuman monsters

Sherlin Hendrick (bottom right)
Anxiety Rabbit

Through the daily practice of intuitive painting, I discovered that my inner voice was weaving its way into my finished artworks as well. In my studio, I allow my intuition to guide me and am often surprised by the results. I may hear a thought, often in the form of a question, inviting exploration. *I wonder what would happen if I added this?* or *How would this color look here?* These intuitive prompts lead my paintings on unexpected journeys, and I never know where they'll end up. For instance, in my painting *Beautiful Dangerous*, I started with the idea of painting a girl sitting on a chair in nature, but as I worked, I noticed myself wondering what it would look like if the earth was writing with colorful patterned snakes. I tried out the idea, and the snakes completely make the painting.

This process of daily intuitive paintings will move energy that is stuck in the body, generate ideas for future work and build a strong connection to your intuition, which will guide you in your own practice.

Kristy Gordon
Beautiful Dangerous

assignment

Your assignment this week is to reconnect your creativity with a childlike sense of wonder and play. Start doing intuitive paintings daily and continue them throughout this course. This can count toward your 25 minutes a day. Spend just 5 to 10 minutes doing a quick intuitive painting as you start your daily creative work. Use whatever medium or surface resonates with you the most. I personally find working on white craft paper on the floor evokes a childlike sense of play.

There are two types of intuitive painting that you can explore. The first is more image-based and is a good way to generate ideas for your work, and the second is more feeling-based and is a powerful way to shift fears and limiting beliefs stuck in the body (which you identified last week). The limiting beliefs you uncovered in last week's lesson could be worked through in intuitive paintings.

To watch a video I made about this fun and easy process go to:

www.kristygordon.com/book-bonuses.

PART 1: IMAGE-BASED CREATION

Intuitive painting can be a wonderful source of image and idea generation. Consider these guidelines as you engage with the intuitive painting experience:

❑ **Preparing a Sacred Space: Create a sacred area to work, whether you work while set up on the floor, on the wall or sitting and working in a sketchbook. Prepare the space however you like. Some people like to burn incense, while others might ring a bell. It's good to turn off any noise like the TV, radio or even music and find some quiet time to work. If other people are around, let them know you won't be able to talk during this process.**

❑ **Color Calling: Tune in to identify the color that is calling out to you to start with.**

❑ **First Thought Best Thought: What is the very first, possibly silly thought that flashed into your mind about the first shape or mark you'd like to make? Do it! Notice how you instantly question it. Do it anyway!**

❑ **Continue Listening: Progress with each mark intuitively, following each thought without questioning it.**

❑ **Inspiration: Notice if any art you've seen is coming to your mind. You're free to draw inspiration from anything that's coming to you.**

❑ Detaching from Judgment: Notice how you're feeling about your creation. Are you starting to judge it with your inner critic? Remind yourself that the goal isn't to make it look "good" in the traditional sense.

❑ Save and Reflect: Once your intuitive painting is completely dry, roll it up and save it so that you can unroll all your intuitive paintings to look through whenever you like. For instance, it can be helpful to look through these when you're trying to come up with ideas for a new piece or when you want to add something to a current piece but don't know what to add.

PART 2: RELEASING TRAPPED ENERGY

Intuitive painting can also be a powerful ritual to help release fears, blocks and limiting beliefs that are being stored in the body as stuck energy. These suggestions will help you move trapped energy:

❑ Body Awareness: Recall a fear or a block that you want to overcome and tune in to your body to locate any areas of tightness that you are unconsciously avoiding breathing into. Ask this area what color and shape it is.

❑ Faithful Expression: Do whatever comes to your mind, no matter what.

❑ Observe Judgment: Notice any judgmental thoughts about what you're creating without giving them power to affect the process.

❑ Emotional Awareness: Pay attention to any emotions that come up as you paint. Allow them to flow through your creation.

❑ Lean In: Amplify anything that is coming up, especially if you find yourself wanting to move away from it or fix it.

❑ Do the Unthinkable: Deliberately ruin it, often!

❑ Monitor Energy: Pay attention to your energy. If you're happily painting and then randomly want to stop even though you're enjoying yourself, it could be the inner critic sabotaging your happiness. So, keep working. However, if you feel like you're losing interest, even if you're in the middle of a brushstroke, stop as soon as you feel your energy dropping or feel intuitively that it's complete.

❑ Reflecting on Insights: Take time to consider insights you've gained about your block. Sometimes what we think is our block turns out to be something entirely different.

❑ Journaling: Write about your experience and what you discovered in the process.

BONUS PRACTICE: CONNECTING WITH YOUR BODY'S "YES"

This supplementary practice will connect you with your body's intuitive signals. You can use this to ask yourself questions about your work in progress to see if the answer is yes or no.

- ❑ Quiet Reflection: **Close your eyes, relax your muscles and pay attention to your body.**

- ❑ Body Awareness: **Pay attention to your body's sensations. What parts are you comfortable breathing into, and what parts are you unconsciously avoiding?**

- ❑ Truth and Response: **Now think of a truth. For example, say to yourself, "My name is _____." See how your body feels as you say that.**

- ❑ Falsehood and Response: **Next, think to yourself something you know isn't true. So, say to yourself, "My name is_____," and insert the wrong name.**

- ❑ Identifying Your Body's Signals: **Did you notice how your body felt a sense of openness toward truth while there was a contraction toward falsehood? This is the difference between your body's "yes" and your body's "no."**

WHAT YOU WILL GAIN FROM THIS

Daily intuitive paintings will become a gateway to fresh ideas and epiphanies. They will help you move energy and blocks that are trapped in the body and allow your inner knowing to guide your work.

Over time, you'll learn how to blend your technical training with your imagination, because you'll find that some of your intuitive paintings will become the seeds of ideas for your finished work. To bridge that gap, you'll learn how to take an idea that was intuitively generated and refine it using the skills and knowledge you have about your craft.

Next week, we'll take a look at your artistic goals by exploring the magical power of goal setting and visualization.

> "I found I could say things with color
> and shapes that I couldn't say any other way—
> things I had no words for."
>
> —Georgia O'Keeffe

week

setting magical goals

5

I believe in the magical power of goal setting. This week you'll be making the wish—setting magical goals for yourself and visualizing your future outcome.

> "Man can only receive what he sees himself receiving . . .
> Every great work, every big accomplishment, has been
> brought into manifestation through holding to the vision,
> and often just before the big achievement, comes
> apparent failure and discouragement."
>
> —Florence Scovel Shinn, author of *The Game of Life*

Twenty years ago, I was very depressed. In a desperate attempt to pull myself out of the abyss, I shifted my focus to creating a list of my artistic aspirations. I drew a little black square beside each goal so I could check it off as I accomplished it. Fifteen years later I found that list and did a triple take. Every single dream on that list, even ones that I had completely forgotten about, had become a reality.

What surprised me the most was the goal of pursuing an MFA at New York Academy of Art. I had never gone to art school, and looking back, I didn't remember even knowing about the Academy back then. Astonishingly, I thought I had discovered the Academy years later, yet there it was on my first goals list. I took out my pen and solemnly checked off that goal, officially completing every single goal that my 20-year-old self envisioned. My conviction in the magical power of goal setting was solidified.

I recently embarked on a new list of goals that transcended my initial aspirations. The biggest goal on this list was to be on the cover of an art magazine. As I sat in my tiny bachelor apartment writing my list, I also cut out an image of one of my paintings and taped it to the cover of an art magazine. I had heard that visual aids can influence the subconscious mind, so I left this handmade image of my art on the cover of a magazine out where it would catch my eye each time I passed it.

In her book *The Game of Life*, Florence Scovel Shinn wrote, "The imagination has been called 'The Scissors of The Mind,' and it is ever cutting, cutting, day by day, the pictures man sees there, and sooner or later he meets his own creations in his outer world."

"I dream of painting and then I paint my dream."

–Vincent van Gogh

The steps to manifestation are: Precisely define your desire, visualize yourself within that reality and experience the emotions, take actions in the direction of your dream and finally let it go completely and know that it is coming.

According to Shinn, manifestation also involves the three parts of the mind: the conscious, subconscious and superconscious. The conscious mind observes the world around us and sees no evidence of our goals, so it generates fears and doubts about our ability to achieve it. The conscious mind impresses these doubts upon the subconscious mind, which is the true seat of manifestation. "Whatever man feels deeply or images clearly, is impressed upon the subconscious mind, and carried out in the minutest detail," writes Shinn. The superconscious mind is like Plato's realm of ideals, brimming with our highest aspirations. They flash across our conscious mind as an ideal that seems unattainable.

I believe it is from this realm that our goals emerge already existing, and they occur to our conscious mind as our highest aspirations. We only have power over our conscious mind, and the subconscious just does what it is directed to do, so we need to find a way to impress our dreams upon our subconscious and release all doubts. Vision boards and other visual reminders help impress our dreams upon our subconscious mind.

This is a photo from a solo show I had at Cube Gallery in Ottawa, Canada, which was one of the goals on my list.

"Life is the art of drawing without an eraser."

–John W. Gardner

Kristy Gordon
Beautiful Dangerous installation
at Cube Gallery

"The position of the artist is humble.
He is essentially a channel."

–Piet Mondrian

Kristy Gordon
The Crossing

A life goal for me was to be featured in art magazines, and for years I used visual aids like vision boards and taping my art to the cover of an art magazine. Also, following Molly Barnes' advice in her book *How to Get Hung*, I put up a huge piece of paper on a wall and wrote the names of everyone I met in the art world, drawing lines to connect people who knew each other. I added the names of magazine editors to that web of connections, even though I hadn't met them yet. I'd walk by this growing network of connections every day, so I knew it well. One day a man walked into my studio at New York Academy of Art, and when he told me his name, I recognized it as one of the magazine editors! I excitedly exclaimed that I loved the magazine he edited, and this sparked a connection. Pretty soon I was featured in his magazine! I saw him walk into other students' studios, but they didn't recognize his name, so they missed the opportunity, underscoring the power of focused goal setting.

Through another series of synchronicities, I had also made contact with the editor of *The Artist's Magazine*. I had written to the editor when I heard she was a big fan of an artist I was apprenticing with, to propose an article about my experience studying with this artist. She loved the idea, but for various reasons, the article fell through. I was very disappointed and felt like I would never reach my goal of appearing in art magazines. However, I added her to my art update email list to keep in touch. About 5 years later, I sent out an art update e-newsletter called "Dreams Really Do Come True." I almost passed out with excitement when I got an email response from the magazine editor asking if I'd like to be featured on the cover of the next issue of *The Artist's Magazine*! My years of visualizing finally paid off, and I suddenly found myself being featured in all my favorite magazines!

You'll notice the goals didn't just magically float into my arms. A lot of them took hard work and consistent action. It's really important to highlight this. It's not just manifestation. On the contrary, manifesting should inspire hard work to fulfill the goal. I'm convinced part of the power of goal setting and visualization is to remove the mental blocks we create when we think it's not possible. Where we might otherwise be apathetic and give up, because of our goals, we take those actions again and again until we achieve the results.

Kristy Gordon
The Artist's Magazine cover, September 2015

That's how getting into magazines was for me. I couldn't figure out how to do it, so I talked to people who had, connected with magazine editors, memorized their names, added them on Facebook and to my mailing list, sent them article proposals and did everything I could think of. The hard work set the foundation, but the ultimate miracle came to me in a most unexpected way after I had let go.

The artist Manu Saluja advises, "Be committed but unattached. Practice being steadfast in pursuing goals while letting go of an overattachment to the outcome." This is important because sometimes when we want something badly, it can block its actual manifestation. When we release our desires, we allow the synchronicities to flow to us. Florence Scovel Shinn writes that when we can "wish without worrying," each dream will be instantaneously fulfilled. Napoleon Hill's counsel "Don't stop three feet from gold" reminds us that we're often closer than we think. By remembering that it is often darkest before the dawn, we can hold faith and keep moving toward our dreams even when we see no evidence. "A big demonstration is often preceded by tormenting thoughts," writes Shinn.

Manu Saluja
Wisdom

There is a four-step process to working with goals and visualization. The first is to write down every single art goal you have. Then visualize your attainment of it and feel the emotions you'll have when it's a reality. The next step is to take any and all actions you can think of in the direction of your goals. The final step is to let go of it completely, almost forgetting about it, while in the back of your mind holding the goal and stay alert for an opening to act on your desire and receive it!

Michelle Doll
Family Portrait (Miller-Vargas)

So what dreams do you have? Would you like to show your work in galleries or have a solo show? Do you want to grow a large social media following or appear in art magazines? Or perhaps you really want to make a living off your art and get commissions. Or maybe you want it all!

Envision yourself having the artistic life you want. Picture it fully: Close your eyes, picture yourself walking into the gallery, seeing your work on the walls, opening a magazine that has your work in it, selling your work to a collector, getting commissions and maybe even having a huge social media account that opens up all sorts of artistic opportunities for you.

Some artists like Michelle Doll even use their art as way to meditate on their desires. Michelle says at one point she was creating paintings as a cathartic expression of her sadness and trauma, but she started to feel that magnified those negative experiences. So she shifted her focus to painting the dreams she wanted to experience, like in her painting *Family Portrait (Miller-Vargas)*; she considered, "What does safety, love and connection feel like? How can I experience tenderness and comfort? How could I not only visualize this but experience those sensations through the act of painting?"

Stuart Wilde, the author of *Miracles*, says it's important to maintain silence when we're manifesting our miracles. Talking about it disperses the energy and also allows doubt to creep in. I've found that to be absolutely true. As soon as I tell someone else about the big wild idea I'm manifesting, I feel I have to defend it to them. So don't tell anyone about your goals until they've manifested! I find that with smaller dreams and goals it can be okay to tell our closest friends, loved ones and partners, but with the big goals, especially ones we doubt we can accomplish, it's best (if possible) not to tell anyone. You can experiment

Buket Savci
Suspended in a Sunbeam

with this, but I can always tell when I shouldn't be sharing a dream: when I tell someone something and immediately feel my ego kick in and want to defend my goal. Then I know I need to stop sharing about it until it's manifested.

I love what Buket Savci says: "Dreams are to be made real! Dream big. Listen to others' advice, but more than that believe in yourself. And keep making your work, not for anybody else, but for yourself."

"An artist is not paid for his labor but for his vision."

—James McNeill Whistler

assignment

Your assignment this week is to spend some time contemplating all your artistic goals, both large and small, and to write them down in checklist form. Next, create a vision board and start to visualize yourself living that life. Then choose a few goals you can start on right away and write down any actions you can take toward them.

PART 1: LIST YOUR GOALS

❑ Take out your journal and list your art goals, drawing a little square box to the left of each one so you can check it off when you accomplish it.

❑ Do you want to show in galleries?

❑ Do you want a large social media account?

❑ Would you love to be a full-time artist making a living entirely from your art?

❑ Do you want to be recognized as an artist in your community?

❑ Is there a class you would like to take?

❑ Is there an art school you would love to attend?

❑ Do you want to appear in art magazines?

❑ Do you want to draw every day, or paint once a week from a live model?

❑ Select a few goals you can start taking action on and write three actions you could take toward making them a reality.

PART 2: CREATE A VISION BOARD

Next, create a vision board detailing all the goals you've set for yourself and start to visualize yourself living the life of your dreams. You can create the vision board by making a collage of cut-up magazines that represent the life you desire. Or you can do comic-like drawings on foam core, which is what I do these days. I like to draw a very happy-looking image of myself doing the things I desire, like holding the magazine in my hands and seeing my work in it. These don't need to be great drawings; mine are like stick figures. The important thing is the emotional content. I just get really happy and draw the happiest, most excited version of me achieving my goals that I can draw. You can do whatever method you prefer. I like to work on a large 22 x 28-inch (56 x 71-cm) piece of foam core and then leave it out where I will see it regularly. Close your eyes and spend some time imagining how it would feel to live this life.

WHAT YOU WILL GAIN FROM THIS

This exercise will guide your future actions, providing fuel for your artistic practice as well as the pursuit of your artistic dreams. You will find yourself feeling more motivated to take action toward your dreams and goals because you are excited by this vision of the life you're creating for yourself. The more you see this magic working, the more confidence you will gain in the magical power of goal setting.

Be sure you check off each goal as you accomplish it. This is a powerful signal to the subconscious mind that goal setting works, and it will give you the confidence to keep moving toward your dreams!

week

brainstorming
with
thumbnails

6

Living in a world that's overloaded with constant stimuli, we often find ourselves either overwhelmed with too many ideas for our art or entirely devoid of them. This information overload can be petrifying, and when it's time to start a new work of art, we may find ourselves at a loss. This week we're going to look at an important part of the creative process: brainstorming with thumbnails.

"In the first phase of the creative process, we are to be completely open, collecting anything we find of interest.... We're searching for potential starting points that can grow into something beautiful."

—Rick Rubin, *The Creative Act*

If you've ever felt like you have no ideas or struggled under the pressure of having too many ideas, this exercise will bring an end to that pain. You'll be creating a database of concepts by doing thumbnails, which are quick sketches, so that you'll be able to refer to your sketchbook whenever you want to start a new work of art.

As we sketch out our ideas, we are also working out their compositions, sometimes doing multiple sketches of the same idea until we have developed one that really works.

I first became aware of the importance of composition while I was landscape painting outdoors in Utah with Jeremy Lipking. He absolutely blew my mind by telling me that composition is one of the most important aspects to painting and that it's a forgotten art. He explained barely anyone understands how to design a painting and hardly anyone can teach it. He even said a somewhat poorly executed painting can look amazing with a strong composition while a beautifully rendered painting can look weak if it lacked a strong compositional design.

Jeremy Lipking
Riders Under Vermilion Cliffs

I immediately worried that my work fell into the second camp. He was right; most artists don't really understand how to design a painting, and there aren't that many good books on it. So it tends to get swept over in art schools.

Observing Jeremy Lipking in action, I saw the power of strong design skills. We were painting the same scene, but his selective design of elements resulted in a beautifully orchestrated masterpiece. Jeremy cleverly heightened contrast in key areas and strategically added or removed details, directing the viewers' gaze masterfully around the painting. The result was an absolutely stunning representation of reality. In contrast, I selected an area of the landscape in front of us, then faithfully copied that view, and my painting looked a bit boring. It became clear I needed to master the art of composition.

That was when I started brainstorming with thumbnails before beginning a painting. I first learned about thumbnails when studying animation at Algonquin College. We were told to loosely sketch out our ideas for a scene, establishing the basic placement of elements in tiny sketches, which our teacher explained were called thumbnails because they were small (like your thumbnail). We didn't do them quite that small, perhaps 3 x 4 inches (8 x 10 cm). They were supposed to be rough, so we left out all the details and focused on how the elements would be composed together. You can see in my thumbnail of *Artificial Light* how rough it is but how it also clearly worked out the composition. It acted like a skeleton for the structure of the finished painting.

Many artists do rough thumbnails before they begin their final painting. These quick sketches can be a way to record an idea and also a tool to work out the composition before investing a lot of time on the finished piece. By doing daily thumbnails, we explore many ideas, allowing us to be less precious about our sketches and get the idea out quickly.

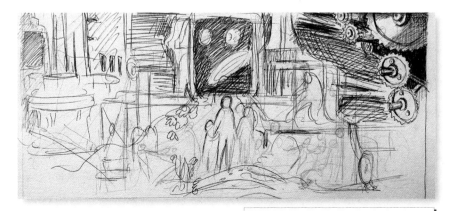

Kristy Gordon
Artificial Light thumbnail

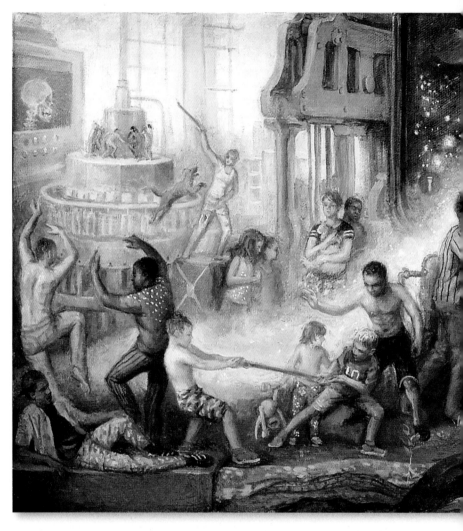

"A good artist has less time than ideas."

–Martin Kippenberger

Kristy Gordon
Artificial Light

Casey Baugh
Game of Love

When we first attempt to sketch out our ideas, we frequently find that we're not that good at it. It's hard, and we may want to avoid it. With time, this practice builds our mental muscles for envisioning and arranging elements. The more we do our daily thumbnails, the more ideas flow and the better we get at designing compositions. Soon we have an entire sketchbook full of ideas for which we have laid the foundation.

Casey Baugh explains, "When you walk into a gallery or museum and glance around at all the paintings, the one that catches your eye does so because of composition." Casey captures the essence of his compositions before he begins a painting in what he describes as "tiny little scribbles," which is exactly how I feel about my thumbnails.

One of the best ways to understand composition is to study the composition of a painting you admire. During my undergraduate years, I did a small oil study of Steven Assael's painting *D* to try to figure out what he was doing compositionally. The more I studied it, the more I was blown away by how each element fit together perfectly. Years later, interviewing Steven on my podcast revealed that his process involved "a scribble" from his imagination to establish the flow of the figures, before having models pose for him from life as he created the painting.

Steven Assael
D © Steven Assael, courtesy of Forum
Gallery, New York, NY

> "[One] paints with the brain and not with the hands."
>
> —Michelangelo

Kristy Gordon (top)
The Annointment

Kristy Gordon (bottom)
The Annointment thumbnails

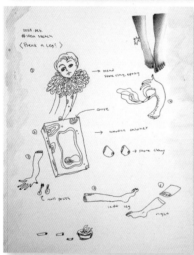

Ailyn Lee (top)
Break a Leg

Ailyn Lee (bottom)
Idea sketch of *Break a Leg*

When I got serious about finding my artistic voice, I challenged myself to do one thumbnail a day, exploring an idea for a painting. Initially, I did these in Sharpie markers, which helped me focus on the arrangement of light and dark shapes in the composition. Later I did these small sketches in graphite colored pencils, felt pens or even gouache. I made it fun. Some of my thumbnails literally looked like scribbles, and others were more refined. I filled up my sketchbook with different ideas for paintings.

Not confined to 2D visual artists, preliminary rough sketches assist artists in all disciplines. Writers and musicians sometimes block out the basics of their art as well. Ailyn Lee creates tiny sketches of her sculptures, and Sherlin Hendrick creates tiny maquettes before creating the final sculpture. Sherlin says, "What surprises me in doing maquettes is I've actually captured the expression in a tiny maquette and then taken out my calibers thinking the expression is just right, to re-create it in the final sculpture."

Nouhaïla Zayane, one of the graduates of an online art program I teach, says she entered the program with no ideas and was so frustrated that her art felt inauthentic she was on the verge of abandoning her painting practice. Nouhaïla says by brainstorming with thumbnails, she identified recurring elements in her sketches that led to a breakthrough in finding her voice.

By developing a sketchbook full of ideas and doing the preliminary work to establish the arrangement of elements, you'll have a database of ideas to draw from, and your final artworks will have a stronger design.

Sherlin Hendrick (top)
Jackal & Hide

Sherlin Hendrick (bottom)
Jackal & Hide maquette

assignment

This week, you will start doing one thumbnail each day. To develop a better understanding of how to create strong compositions, I suggest you start by doing a few thumbnails that analyze the compositions of your favorite works of art. After that, sketch out the arrangement of elements each day for one of your own ideas.

Often, you'll spend only 5 to 10 minutes on each thumbnail. They don't need to be refined; they just need to get the ideas out in a way that you can start to explore them visually. Here are the two types to try:

❑ **Analyze Masterworks: Start by doing three thumbnails studying the compositional arrangement of three of your favorite works of art. Do these in black and white. I like to use Sharpie markers to keep them simple.**

❑ **Daily Exploration: Progress to daily thumbnails where you'll brainstorm fresh ideas and refine the composition for your own artistic concepts.**

For each thumbnail remember to:

❑ **Frame Your Vision: If you're a 2D visual artist, draw a border around your thumbnail that represents the canvas or paper you're working on. Will you compose the picture horizontally, vertically or make a diptych or triptych?**

❑ **Focal Point: Select a clear center of interest as the main focal point of your sketch.**

❑ **Arrange the Elements: Sketch the elements in your piece.**

❑ **Guide the Movement: Design the movement of the eyes throughout the art.**

❑ **Pattern of Light and Dark: Consider the arrangement of light and dark shapes.**

- ❑ Create Balance: **Balance the piece from left to right and top to bottom, either symmetrically or asymmetrically.**

- ❑ Edge Consideration: **Pay attention to the edges, ensuring nothing is directing the eye out of the picture, and instead, design the elements to hold the eye within the picture.**

- ❑ Play with Mediums: **Do some in black and white to design the arrangement of dark and light shapes, and try some in color with pencil crayons, felt pens or paint. Have fun with it!**

WHAT YOU WILL GAIN FROM THIS

This exercise will help get the ideas flowing. You won't feel so frozen and overwhelmed about having an idea and not knowing how to execute it. Instead, you will just start scribbling around to find some sort of flow and then do more thumb-nails until you've got your idea worked out. Do these daily sketches and you will find that more and more ideas come to you. You will also have a database of ideas you can draw from every time you want to start something new!

Next week, we will look at knowing your world and understanding the language of your medium of choice!

"Creativity is allowing yourself to make mistakes. Art is knowing which ones to keep."

—Scott Adams

week

knowing your world

7

This week, we'll dive into the important topic of understanding how our art fits into the broader picture of what's being created around us. Knowing your world is about being up to date on art news and happenings, understanding the history of your art style and medium and gaining technical proficiency in it.

"Being informed isn't necessarily about defending your own work but just being aware of the issues that are current, and basically not making a fool of yourself if you're in conversation."

—Peter Drake

By immersing yourself in every aspect of your art world, you are open to it and always filling your brain with it, while also staying up to date on current trends and discussions. For instance, if you are a painter and you know both the cultural context you are painting in and the ways others have done it before you, you can make informed decisions in the most thoughtful way. And you never know what success might come from a simple conversation where you really wowed someone.

The artist Jacob Hicks explains the balance between freedom and being informed perfectly when he's teaching children's art classes at Queens Museum. He says, "There are so many places in your life where you're going to be told what to do or how to do something. With art, this is your universe; you are in control. This is where you have freedom."

Jacob explains he's also obsessed with the long history of painting, and he does think there are good paintings and bad paintings. He uses this understanding to consider if something conforms to what is historically "good" as he creates his work. Jacob acknowledges that it's a bit of a paradox—this total freedom as well as a historical structure. I personally feel this is what creates great art.

In Jacob's painting *Woman 46* we can see the historical influence in this woman's face, painted like an old Italian master, overlayed with contemporary patterns and colors.

Great artists can contextualize their work in relation to other artists who are aesthetically similar. They know the names of artists who are relevant to them and can describe the ways their art is similar as well as different. This task requires an understanding of both art history and contemporary art, an undertaking that initially completely overwhelmed me.

I started by taking an introductory course to art history and watching movies like Sister Wendy Beckett's *Story of Painting* to get an overview. Then I started to just do a short reading every day on an artist I admired or an article about contemporary art that caught my interest.

Don't get too overwhelmed by this, and don't start to think you have to act pretentious to function in the art world. Being ourselves shows confidence, and the most confident artists are the ones who aren't trying to seem too smart. Just do a little bit of reading every day, and soon enough, you will be surprised by how rooted you are in art history and contemporary art!

Know that your world goes beyond staying informed about current events. As you delve deeper, you discover that the medium you're working in is an entire language. For me, that meant I had to completely understand the language of painting. This concept sounded amazing to me, almost mystical, but I didn't initially understand exactly what it meant. I could tell there was something missing in my work, and I could intuitively feel understanding the language of painting was part of the answer.

Jacob Hicks
Woman 46, God of Small Things

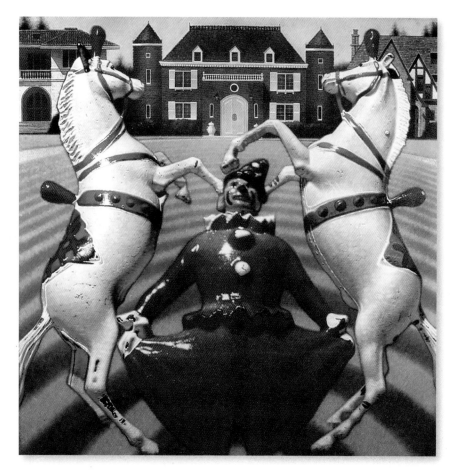

Certain modes of expression bring specific associations and connotations to the work. Peter Drake explains, "The language of Dutch seventeeth-century painting, working with indirect paint, medieval egg tempera or sixties and seventies stain painting traditions, are all languages. They're alive and they come with associations." As you come to understand the language of your medium, the decisions you make and techniques you use enhance the meaning.

Peter Drake
McBroke

Peter Drake describes these languages as carrying "baggage" as well as "real richness," adding layers of meaning to your work. For example, I work in a language of painting that's inspired by old master Renaissance painting, and the baggage this tradition carries is that it was historically a masculine genre. By inserting women and feminine motifs into my art, I'm dismantling gendered hierarchies that have long been a part of our visual culture.

Kristy Gordon
Journey

"Art is a temporal event translated into a spatial object."

—Jerry Saltz

Understanding your medium's language entails a certain proficiency with the technical aspects of your craft. Whether you're a painter, sculptor, installation artist or photographer, mastery of your craft involves honing certain technical skills. For me, this includes rendering form, designing color schemes, composing pictures and creating appealing brushstrokes.

The painter Kyle Staver said once in an interview that color was the last piece to click for her and that a true knowledge of how to create a harmonious color scheme in a painting took a long time to understand. You can see what a beautiful colorist she is in her paintings *Dawn* and *Dusk*. When I read this interview, it suddenly dawned on me that I still didn't understand color. It was the very last piece for me to get, so I started doing daily readings about how to combine colors to create color harmony.

Daily reading about art history and contemporary art, as well as a deliberate study of specific technical aspects of your art form, will contribute to artistic mastery.

"I have invented nothing; I only rediscover."

–Auguste Rodin

Kyle Staver (top)
Dawn

Kyle Staver (left)
Dusk

assignment

Your task this week is to do one daily reading to enhance your knowledge about what's being created around you and to deepen your understanding of your craft. Alternate between the two options to continuously expand your knowledge about your art world and your craft.

OPTION 1: DAILY INTERVIEWS AND ARTICLES

❏ Read one article or interview daily about an artist you admire.

❏ Read articles about how other artists found their artistic voice, which is very helpful.

❏ Consider as you read how your work is similar or different.

❏ Find valuable articles and interviews in publications such as *Art in America*, *Breakfast with ARTNews* and *Hyperallergic*.

❏ Get an overview of art history. A good resource to start with is Sister Wendy Beckett's *The Story of Painting*.

OPTION 2: DAILY CRAFT IMPROVEMENT READING

❏ Identify two areas you'd like to improve technically.

❏ Read an article or watch a video about these areas for improvement related to your craft. You can start by googling these techniques to find something to read.

❏ After a while, you will have read a lot online about the techniques you're researching, so you may like to get some books like the ones I suggest on the next page.

SUGGESTED RESOURCES

- ❑ *Composition: Understanding Line, Notan and Color* by Arthur Wesley Dow

- ❑ *The Painter's Secret Geometry: A Study of Composition in Art* by Charles Bouleau

- ❑ *A Fiber Artist's Guide to Color & Design* by Heather Thomas

- ❑ *Interaction of Color* by Josef Albers

- ❑ *The Elements of Color: A Treatise on the Color System of Johannes Itten Based on His Book the Art of Color* by Johannes Itten

WHAT YOU WILL GAIN FROM THIS

Over time, you will find yourself very well-versed not only in your technical medium, but also in the current trends and discussions within the art world. Your ability to talk about your artistic choices and engage in meaningful conversations about your work will become much easier once you're reading every day.

Next week, we'll look at cultivating a safe container for your art, providing the support you need as you vulnerably uncover your artistic voice.

"The artist is a receptacle for emotions that come from all over the place: from the sky, from the earth, from a scrap of paper, from a passing shape, from a spider's web."

—Pablo Picasso

week

cultivating
a safe
container
for sharing

8

Creating art is often viewed as a solitary pursuit, but the reality is quite different. As artists, we need to navigate two aspects of sharing our work: cultivating supportive relationships with other artists and choosing when to post on social media. This week, we'll delve into the importance of knowing when to share your work and when to keep it hidden.

"The coordination of knowledge and effort between two or more people who work towards a definite purpose in a spirit of harmony. No two minds ever come together without thereby creating a third, invisible intangible force, which may be likened to a third mind."

—Napoleon Hill

Artists throughout history from Picasso and Matisse to van Gogh and Gaugin have formed alliances, regularly sharing and critiquing each other's work. This community aspect is crucial to artistic growth. It inspires new ideas and can create a slight sense of competition that pushes us even further. Making art is such a complex process, and there are so many considerations, which is why gaining insights on how your work is being perceived by other supportive artists is beneficial. It provides a system of checks and balances that is essential for mastering one's craft. My accountability artists played a crucial role in the development of my painting *Centrifuge*, providing insights and feedback as it evolved.

As artists, we all experience moments of self-doubt and procrastination. To overcome these obstacles, we need to cultivate a safe container for our work. Establishing consistent, supportive relationships with fellow artists provides a space to discuss our work, share vulnerabilities and receive feedback.

Understanding our creative process and knowing when to create in solitude and when to seek external input to refine our work is essential. When I first underwent the deep work of consciously exploring my true voice, I had a phase where I stopped showing my art to anyone so that I could develop it away from outside influences. After several months of working in seclusion, I felt like I was working in a vacuum. I needed to find a few artists I really trusted to show this vulnerable new work to. I organized studio visits with Noelle Timmons and Lily Koto Olive, two artists I admired and trusted, and I shared my new work and intentions with them. You can see in the images of their work that they are both working with the figure in imaginative ways, which is why I trusted their opinion about my work.

"Creativity takes courage."

—Henri Matisse

Kristy Gordon (top)
Centrifuge

Noelle Timmons (bottom left)
Jacki's House

Lily Koto Olive (bottom right)
Until Healing Begins

Recognizing the benefit of artistic alliances, I asked two other artists, Manu Saluja and Liz Adams, if they would like to meet regularly to critique each other's work and hold each other accountable. We started emailing each other what we were working on and talking about it over the phone every week. Liz and Manu kept me on track with my artistic goals, gave me honest feedback about my work and became intimately familiar with my intentions for my art. Liz explains, "The work of an artist is mostly done in solitude. But I've found it really helpful to have an objective eye to look at my work along the way. Having someone who knows my work and who I trust to give me honest feedback has become a meaningful part of my artistic process."

They also helped me process the pain of harsh feedback. I remember once when I was crushed by a past collector coming to my art show and lecturing me for hours about everything he didn't like about my new work. I held it together at the show, but afterward I never wanted to paint again. I talked to Manu and Liz about it, and they understood. They had been there before. We all have if we've been on this path for a while. That's the difficult thing about being an artist: Criticism feels so personal. We care so much about our work. If someone says something mean about our art, we can't say, "Oh well, who cares." We might try, but that's not the truth. The truth is we *do* care. We care so much. After harsh criticism we need to tenderly process the pain.

Luckily, I had Liz and Manu as my safety container. Our weekly calls had become my secret weapon to make sure I kept going no matter what. I shared with them that I felt like quitting. Manu said sometimes when she feels like that, she rediscovers joy in just the physical act of painting, forgetting about goals and intentions. The idea of quitting made me so miserable that to comfort myself I decided to just paint only to enjoy the physical act of painting. Slowly I got back into it, and that reinvigorated my artistic practice. Artists know what to say to each other and how to be supportive through difficulties.

When you set up accountability partners, practice being open to their feedback. At first, it can be hard to see their perspective if it differs from yours. Occasionally your accountability artist might suggest something that makes you realize your intention is to go in the opposite direction of what they're suggesting. But almost always, if you sit with their feedback and digest it, you will see they have a point.

Manu Saluja
The Unraveling

Liz Adams
Religieuse aux Framboises

"Don't be an art critic,
but paint,
there lies salvation."

–Paul Cézanne

Aleah Chapin
It Was the Sound of Their Feet

"I would rather die
of passion than die of
boredom."

–Émile Zola

This is in stark contrast to feedback we receive on social media, which can be overwhelming and undereducated, often pushing us toward mediocrity and comfortable norms. The internet and social media, while opening the doors to a broader audience, can also damage a budding artist's self-esteem. The ease of sharing online can lead artists to post before they're ready and can result in comparisons that cause artists to question their talent or shift their intentions before a piece is fully realized. My personal journey led me to step away from posting my work on social media for a year. This gave my artistic voice time to develop away from the public eye. Back then, I had no idea how algorithms worked. I would post my work and only get a few likes while my friends got thousands. I was convinced people didn't like my work. And that's the risk with social media. If the algorithm doesn't deem it a good post, it won't show it to anyone. As artists, we tend to interpret that as a reflection of merit. That's why I decided to stop posting my work. It gave me time in seclusion to develop my voice without external influences.

After a year, I felt confident in my new body of work and that it would serve me to market it more. I was ready to call in new opportunities. I felt clear about my new direction and had completed a series of paintings in my new style. Therefore, posting my newly finished paintings wouldn't affect the direction of the art. I also wanted to make sure that posting a work in progress didn't influence decisions I made, so I made a rule for myself never to post anything until it was basically finished. I take process shots at the beginning, middle and end, and I post all of them, but only after the painting is finished. The key is to find a way to share our work when the time is right, while not letting the sharing interfere with our studio practice.

The artist Aleah Chapin said, "I need to be very private in my studio space. Then when I'm ready, I can put it out there because I've removed myself a little bit from it." Aleah says this helps her be more vulnerable and truer to herself. In Aleah's painting *It Was the Sound of Their Feet*, I get a sense of the supportive community she has found in her family, because this is a painting of her aunties together.

The artist Alonsa Guevara only posts her work on social media once she is sure about exactly where she is going with it. Sometimes she'll post work midway through the process, but only if she's very sure about its direction. When she's working on a new body of work that feels more vulnerable, she does show work privately to a few people she trusts, but she'll wait until she's finished so she's clear about the direction before she posts on social media. In Alonsa's multimedia installation *Ghaf & Migration: Observing the Unknown*, she was going in a slightly new direction, so she didn't post any images on social media until it was finished because she didn't want comments to affect her decision-making process.

By discovering what we need in terms of a supportive community as well as guidelines for ourselves that keep the vulnerability of our practice safe and protected, we can create freely and also show our work when the time is right.

"I paint for myself. I don't know how to do anything else, anyway."

–Francis Bacon

Alonsa Guevara
Ghaf & Migration: Observing the Unknown

assignment

Consider what your creative practice needs so you feel safe and supported. Take out your journal and answer these questions:

- ❑ **Do you need supportive artists whom you check in with regularly to discuss your art?**

- ❑ **Name two artists you could reach out to for regular check-ins.**

- ❑ **Do you need to create your work away from the public eye for a time while you explore your voice?**

- ❑ **At what point in the creative process will you share your work on the internet? (For example, at the beginning, midway through or only when fully finished.)**

- ❑ **Send a text or an email RIGHT NOW (don't wait!) asking your fellow artists and/or friends if they would be interested in being an accountability partner for supporting and critiquing each other's work.**

WHAT YOU WILL GAIN FROM THIS

Developing a safe container for your creative practice will allow you the freedom to work out your creative ideas safely while also being able to show your work at the appropriate time. The supportive artists you include in your safety net will keep you consistently moving toward your goals, helping you to clarify your intentions for your work and ensuring that the decisions you make align with your intentions. They will also provide technical insights that may have escaped your eye. You will find yourself making faster progress and feeling more satisfied with the outcome as a result.

"Art is the stored honey of the human soul."

–Theodore Dreiser

week

turning
ideas into
finished
works

9

Many artists experience frustration the first time they attempt to fuse their ideas and imagination together with the techniques of their craft. This week, we'll delve into the tools and resources necessary to bridge that gap, transforming artistic visions into reality.

> "Art may only exist, and the artist may only evolve,
> by completing the work."
>
> —Rick Rubin, *The Creative Act*

In his book *The Creative Act*, Rick Rubin describes the "seed phase," where ideas are collected without constraints. After freely exploring our ideas, the process shifts, and a sense of direction develops, marking our shift into the "craft phase." Although less glamorous and exciting, this phase is essential for bringing an artwork to completion.

Let me tell you a story of a time I needed help bringing an idea to life. When I took on the challenge of translating one of my intuitive paintings into a huge 5 x 8-foot (1.5 x 2.5-m) oil painting called *The Cosmic Lotus*, it was very frustrating because I literally didn't know how to do it. I had no system.

I started by reproducing the essence of my intuitive painting (which we learned about in Week 4 [page 54]) on the giant canvas. To fill the gaps in my imagination as I roughly mapped in various elements, I turned to several resources such as personal photos, online images (being mindful of copyright) and inspiration from historical artworks. By coming back to my practice of knowing my world and looking at historical works (which we learned about in Week 7 [page 92]), I was able to gain inspiration to help me crystallize my vision and lay the foundation.

Kristy Gordon
Surrender

Next, I breathed life into my figures by working with live models, having my friends pose for me as I captured nuances and details that photos couldn't convey. I picked flowers on my daily walks and even collected dead insects to set up still lifes in my studio for details. I found that adding elements that were painted from life enhanced my paintings.

Kristy Gordon
Liminality

"I saw the angel in the marble and carved until I set him free."

—Michelangelo

Kristy Gordon (top)
The Cosmic Lotus

Kristy Gordon
Plasticine model as reference for
The Cosmic Lotus

This idea of painting from life means rather than painting from photos, painters have people pose for them live in their studio or set up still lifes of flowers and other elements from real objects. This enables them to capture more nuance than they can when they work from photos. I make more confident brushstrokes when I work from life and also capture more color variation. However, because I'm also painting images that don't exist, I need to blend every tool imaginable to create a scene. You might find that you will need to use the various tools, too, finding things that work for you to help you achieve your artistic aims.

For instance, I hit a roadblock with *The Cosmic Lotus* when painting the horses, especially their cast shadows on the ground. Inspired by Renaissance artists who made models as references, I went to the kids' store and bought some colored plasticine and toy horses. I sculpted choppy-looking figures with the plasticine, placed them on the toy horses and illuminated them to create bold shadow patterns. Working from life, whether from live models or makeshift figurines, allows me to resolve any issues in a painting, making alterations until I achieve a carefully constructed realization of my idea.

Over time, I developed other techniques such as photographing people from above while they lay on the ground for flying figures. I also found I could use colored transparencies such as an orange film over a light to replicate the lighting of an explosion or fire illuminating a model. I even bought a poseable Halloween skeleton as reference for the dancing skeletons and discovered that I could paint at the American Museum of Natural History, combining various elements—animals, insects and other creatures—to create the hybrid and mystical beings in my artwork.

Gradually I uncovered creative ways to get the references I needed. The completion of *The Cosmic Lotus* marked not only the transformation of an idea into a finished work of art, but also a personal transformation. I started out as a person who couldn't create such a painting, and over the course of completing it, I became a person who could.

> "As practice makes perfect, I cannot but make progress; each drawing one makes, each study one paints, is a step forward."
>
> —Vincent van Gogh

Patricia Watwood
Femen Flora

"A painting is never finished—it simply stops in interesting places."

—Paul Gardner

Like many artists, it was frustrating and challenging when I first merged my ideas with my painting techniques. Patricia Watwood's solution to create setups in her studio that were as close as possible to her vision resonated with my journey. She even printed large cloud photos to hang behind her model to capture subtle relationships between figure and ground.

Each artist must discover for themselves the tools and resources they will use to be able to bring an idea from their imagination to harmonious completion. Many artists draw inspiration from a range of images related to their background as well as art history. For instance, Naruki Kukita blended references from Jacques-Louis David's painting *The Death of Marat*, Edvard Munch's painting *Puberty* as well as Japanese anime that he had seen growing up in Japan to create his painting *The Death of Virtual Marat*.

Artist Alicia Brown said, "I always had a voice, but I didn't have the technical skills or the tools necessary to share the stories that I wanted to share."

Naruki Kukita
The Death of Virtual Marat

Alicia Brown
Citizen in the Promise Land

Some artists build elaborate models. Amy Bennett creates models of the urban settings that she paints. Sculptor Ron Lambert sometimes makes maquettes of his sculptures to test their functionality, and other artists use 3D modeling programs to provide the references they need to realize their ideas.

Amy Bennett
Flirt

Amy Bennett
Model for *Packages*

Successful manifestation requires both the visionary and the integrator. The visionary imagines the idea, and the integrator brings it into existence. The diversity of tools, such as hiring live models, creating models and maquettes, referencing photos and using 3D modeling programs, supports our artistic voice, allowing a harmonious union between our imagination and our ability to realize the idea and bring it to a successful completion.

In the finishing phase I always remind myself that "It doesn't have to be perfect; it just has to be finished." Artists can get so caught up in perfectionism they never complete anything. The key is to finish our works of art, learning and evolving with each completion.

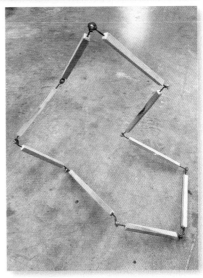

Ron Lambert
Ossify

Ron Lambert
Ossify **maquette**

assignment

This week, your assignment is to explore diverse avenues to supplement your imagination and bring your ideas to fruition. The goal is to take an idea from imagination all the way through to completion, no matter how long it takes, exploring the available tools to see what works for you.

Here are some paths to explore:

❑ **Make models with plasticine and light them to get convincing colors and shadow patterns.**

❑ **Hire a live model or have your friends over to take the poses required for the artwork.**

❑ **Look at historical and contemporary art, drawing inspiration from diverse sources.**

❑ **Utilize kids' toys and light them to match your artwork's lighting and mood.**

❑ **Transform online images into unique references, ensuring no copyright infringement.**

❑ **Visit a museum with a focused question about your artwork, and look for answers in the work you see.**

❑ **Do a photoshoot of yourself or a friend to capture the required poses.**

❑ **Reference still frames from a public domain movie.**

Choose at least three methods from this list and see how you can incorporate them into your practice. Each tool will act as a bridge between the boundless flow of your imagination and the structured logic of your craft.

WHAT YOU WILL GAIN FROM THIS

These exercises empower you to bridge the gap between conception and creation, building confidence in your ability to bring any idea to completion with the right tools. You will discover the abundance of references available, reinforcing the belief that with time and these tools, you can realize any creative vision.

Discovering the tools and processes to bring an idea to completion will help you make adjustments to a work, allowing you to identify flaws in execution and giving you the ability to resolve any issues. Making maquettes, working with live models, using photo references and referencing historical works of art will help you bring an idea from your brain to the physical world.

"The object isn't to make art, it's to be in that wonderful state which makes art inevitable."

—Robert Henri

week

opening to epiphanies in your art

10

Taking your work from good to great sometimes requires a leap of faith. Experiencing an epiphany that guides your work is one of the most magical and exciting experiences of being an artist.

> "When you can do the common things of life in an uncommon way, you will command the attention of the world."
>
> —George Washington Carver

Imagine you've been diligently working on a project, and while it's looking good, it's not yet "eye-popping." Then suddenly you get an idea. Do you try it? You might risk ruining what good you've created, but this risk might be the very thing that elevates your creation to the level of genius.

I remember working on a painting of people seen from behind in water—a representation of unity and collective consciousness. After meticulously rendering their backs and striving for perfection, I had an idea that was way out there. I envisioned a strange circle on the horizon line in interference blue, which is kind of like magical paint that from one angle almost disappears, but from another angle is a shimmery blueish silver. Logically, the idea made no sense. Was the circle a sun? Was it sacred geometry? I had no idea. At the risk of ruining my nearly completed work, I took a breath and carefully painted a circle on the horizon line. I loved it. It absolutely transformed the painting, adding an esoteric touch that made it truly unique.

Our creative genius, which Elizabeth Gilbert describes as being akin to a magical fairy that lives outside of ourselves, serves as the course of ideas for our art. In *The Creative Act*, Rick Rubin describes the universe as one big creative act, with countless moments of inspiration happening within each of us. This concept emphasizes that our creative impulses are guided by the larger creative force of the universe. We don't always understand why we're getting the creative inspiration that we are, but this universe is guiding us, just as it's guiding everything.

This mystical state of inspiration, akin to channeling, can manifest unexpectedly during dreams, walks, baths or visits to art museums. I remember a pivotal moment during my undergrad

when an epiphany in a dream gave me the solution to a problem for an arched wooden frame I was trying to craft for a Barbie painting. Despite being told it was impossible, I persisted through months of experimentation with modeling paste and hand carving. One night, I dreamt of using these half-wooden dowels from a hardware store, effortlessly bending them and gluing them onto my panel. It worked like a charm in my dream, and I woke up knowing it would work in reality, too—and it did!

Kristy Gordon (top)
I Am-We Are

Kristy Gordon (left)
Barbie as a Saint

"The world of reality has its limits; the world of imagination is boundless."

—Jean-Jacques Rousseau

"Great art picks up where nature ends."

–Marc Chagall

Michela Martello
Prophecy Garden

The artist Michela Martello also describes her creative process as "like channeling something that comes from another dimension." She says, "There are a lot of internal demons—internal fears and insecurities that are part of my creation process." And she combines those with what she calls divine inspiration that sometimes comes to her in dreams, to create "a cathartic manifestation as an artwork."

Author Sam Horn defines the creative voice as an amalgamation of our "experience, expertise and epiphanies." I've found that epiphanies often emerge when I'm least focused on my art—during walks, baths or other moments of relaxation. In fact, one of the best ways to connect with our intuition is to distract ourselves. This calms us enough so the ego releases its grip on us and allows ideas to flow. It's often when our mind is relaxed and we're not thinking about our art that epiphanies emerge.

Sometimes epiphanies strike when I'm at art museums or galleries. My eye will feel guided to a beautiful composition, a particular edge quality or a certain color scheme, and suddenly I'll realize that I could incorporate similar aspects into a piece that I'm working on. I experienced this when I was working on *Interconnected*. I had developed the overall placement of elements and was painting details, but the painting felt like it was lacking something compositionally. It wasn't eye-popping, and I suspected it had to do with a lack of clarity around the arrangement of light and dark shapes.

While visiting the Metropolitan Museum of Art, I held this vague question in mind: "How can I resolve this painting?" I then saw a Rembrandt painting called *The Toilet of Bathsheba* (turn to the next page to see this painting). I was immediately struck by the glowing lightness of the nude figure's skin contrasted by the dark environment around her, as well as the arrangement of other light shapes, such as the opening to sky behind her, which guided the eye around the painting. I became immediately curious what the effect would be if I lightened the figure in my painting and darkened the environment around her. I eagerly tried it as soon as I got home and felt a sense of relief; the issue had been resolved and the painting now felt right.

Epiphanies also come when we're engaged in our creative work. Often they come in the form of subtle questions like, "I wonder what will happen if I try this?" Sometimes these seem to come from nowhere and other times, they're inspired by something we've seen in our daily lives. These inner nudges come quietly, like our still, small voice, so we have to be very attentive and listen carefully to these inner questions. Sam Horn writes, "Ink it when you think it." Writing down these intuitive impressions gives more voice to them, allowing us to notice them more and take action.

> "Painting is a means of self-enlightenment."
>
> —John Olsen

"Art is a collaboration between God and the artist, and the less the artist does the better."

—André Gide

Kristy Gordon (top left)
Interconnected

Rembrandt van Rijn (bottom left)
The Toilet of Bathsheba

Julia Jenkins (top right)
Solar Sorceress

The transformative impact of following epiphanies is something that one of my students, Julia Jenkins, has experienced. Midway through painting *Solar Sorceress*, she had an epiphany. She had been watching a show called *The Universe: Secrets of the Sun* and realized that something felt like it was missing. To her, the painting represented self-empowerment and magic that she felt could be expressed more powerfully if the woman was holding an actual sun instead of a crystal ball. It's a good thing she followed her inner guidance, because the world loved it, too! The reel of it she posted on Instagram went viral, garnering 5 million views and 10,000 new followers, as well as new commissions. But most importantly, that painting became the first one where Julia knew she had found her artistic voice. One key factor in that painting was a mystical sense of lighting that was coming from the sun, which she echoed in her next painting *The Alchemist* with the green glow coming from the magical concoctions the alchemist is holding.

I think of it as following our excitement—looking for things that, as Marie Kondo wrote, "spark joy" in us.

Now that you have been creating for 25 minutes a day, you will now be creating space for a work to incubate and evolve. This leaves room for epiphanies to enter into your art. You won't be exhausting yourself with endless hours of aimless work, but instead you'll

Julia Jenkins
The Alchemist

approach each session with clear intentions. You'll find that when you're not working, your mind will be subconsciously grappling with unresolved questions about your art. If you're attentive, you might get signs from the universe or epiphanies that guide the progression of the work. You probably won't get an epiphany for every work of art, and that's okay, as not every piece needs one to be great or something you are satisfied with. However, by consistently engaging with your work and the creative process, your creative genius will feed you more and more with these magical epiphanies, and as you open up to epiphanies, they can guide the direction of your work as well as the development of your artistic voice.

assignment

Pick a piece that you're working on, and clarify what you feel is lacking or presents a problem or unresolved issue. For example, does a painting lack that "wow" factor? Do you feel like there is a lack of color harmony? Whatever the unresolved issue you have identified, hold that in your mind as you go about your life. Then pay attention to what presents itself to you. Do you get a curiosity while watching a show that could enhance your piece? Or do you see art in a museum that has a color scheme that mesmerizes you? When a magical insight arrives, write it down immediately. Here are other things you can do:

❏   **Set an intention when you go to bed at night to have a dream that answers your art-related questions.**

❏   **Try forgetting about your art-related questions and go for a walk, take a bath, cook a nice meal or clean your space. Sometimes your best ideas will come when you relax and let go.**

❏   **Set an intention to be guided to certain ideas in your day-to-day life that will help resolve a piece.**

❏   **Try putting the piece you're working on aside for a time and begin something new while you wait for guidance on the next steps to the work in question.**

❏   **Carry a notepad with you or use a note-taking app on your phone to record any intuitive nudges and epiphanies. If you think you might be having an epiphany, write it down.**

❏   **Keep in mind the components of your voice that you identified in Week 1 (page 20), and notice any epiphanies that arise about how to incorporate those elements into your art.**

WHAT YOU WILL GAIN FROM THIS

This exploration will yield epiphanies on seamlessly merging your imagination with the technical aspects of your craft. You'll also get mind-blowing ideas that will take an artwork from good to great and create something that's truly unique and exciting. The more you connect with your intuition and notice epiphanies, the more they will come to you, in all aspects of your art and career. They will become a guiding force showing you the way to make your art and professional dreams come true!

week

transforming
the new
routine into
a habit

11

You're nearing the end of the course, and if you've done the exercises, however imperfectly, for 11 weeks, you've created a new habit and have uncovered your own unique artistic expression. This week is about cementing this new routine into a lifelong habit and developing a plan of action for moving forward with your artistic goals.

"Great things are done by a series of small things
brought together."

—Vincent van Gogh

If you have done this course diligently, then you've probably faced bumps and challenges along the way. You may feel like you've done it imperfectly, but you can't do it wrong. Letting go of our perfectionism is a huge part of allowing our true voice to emerge. Whatever has come is as it should be. Transformation is never an easy process, and authentic self-expression is often vulnerable.

The key now is to take the tools you've learned and the momentum you've gained and continue them in your regular practice. This is also a good time to take stock of your current goals both artistically and in terms of your art career. Make a list of your current top five goals and break them into five tiny action steps that lead toward each goal. This will help you stay motivated and give you a path of action as you work.

Consider which tools were most helpful to you and what their role will be in your practice moving forward. Will you continue to do the daily brain-drain writing as I have? Does it serve you to set a goal to do an intuitive painting daily or weekly? Would you benefit from brainstorming with thumbnails on a regular basis? What will be your research intentions in terms of knowing your art world? Each artist will find different ways to integrate all these tools into their practice.

The most pivotal exercise for me has been painting for 25 minutes a day, no matter what. This commitment has enabled me to push through artistic blocks, move past disappointments and hear the inner calling of my intuition guiding me as I work. This daily habit allows us to notice patterns emerging over time, such as our interest in a particular subject. It's also how we can hear the still, small voice of our intuition guiding us as we work.

With time you will find that some of the actions evolve. I initially did one intuitive painting a day and worked large-scale (like we talked about in Week 4 [page 54]), and after a while, I started doing intuitive paintings less regularly and incorporating intuition into my finished paintings by opening to epiphanies in my work (like we learned about in Week 10 [page 126]). I continued the targeted daily readings on technique (which you identified in Week 7 [page 92]) for about a year, and when

I had a solid understanding, I shifted from daily art-related reading to regularly attending art show receptions to stay connected to my community. I still do daily brain-drain writing, often in the morning, and it had changed (and saved!) my artistic life. I continued doing thumbnails every day for about a year, so I have sketchbooks full of ideas I can look through whenever I need them. I just finished two paintings that literally came to me as if they were channeled (from a couple of brainstorming sessions) in my sketchbook. I think they are my favorite paintings yet. I also still sketch out a rough thumbnail before beginning any final painting.

Kristy Gordon
Map of the Universe installation at The Gallery at Greenly Center

Kristy Gordon
Map of the Universe sketch

Artist Dina Brodsky, who recommends people create a daily sketchbook habit, says, "At first, your sketchbook practice might be awkward, and feel like another part of your to-do list, but it will become more fluid. After a week or two, you'll find yourself looking forward to time with your book, as with practice, it becomes more of an extension of your mind." This is how the new habits that you are creating for yourself will be. Once you're clear about what habits you want to carry forward in your life and with what frequency, spend some time considering when these actions will fit best in your day.

The secret to being a successful artist is to stay in the game for a really long time. That is why in Week 8 (page 102) you developed supportive relationships with other artists to help you stay committed for the long haul. If you stay in it long enough, you will see the results.

While some claim it takes 21 days to create a new habit, this can vary from person to person, and also from task to task. You've dedicated 11 weeks to finding your voice, and you've seen the benefits. For most, this timeframe will have created new habits and begun to completely transform their artistic lives.

Kristy Gordon (left)
As Above So Below

Kristy Gordon (above top)
As Above So Below sketch

Dina Brodsky (above bottom)
Sketchbook

"The artist is nothing
without the gift,
but the gift is nothing
without work."

—Émile Zola

You'll find that as you reach the completion of this program, the actions might shift slightly as they integrate more into your daily life, and the goal now is to find a sustainable pace for you to carry the tools forward into your ongoing artistic practice while also carving out a path to move toward your artistic goals.

assignment

Now that you've cultivated the habit of a daily artistic practice and had a profound artistic transformation, it's time to create a plan of action for integrating these habits into regular art practice and plotting out a course of action to move forward on your current artistic goals.

Take out your notebook and journal about all you've learned and are feeling right now, to cement the ideas you've learned so far. Next, write about how you are feeling in your career and path as an artist. Create a weekly schedule that you will commit to and make note of the following:

PART 1: INTEGRATING THE TOOLS

❑ **Which tool was the most helpful and groundbreaking for you?**

❑ **How much time will you commit to your creative projects each day?**

❑ **How often will you do the brain-drain writing moving forward?**

❑ **What regular actions will you take to continue to evolve your knowledge of your art world?**

❑ **When or how often will you do an intuitive painting?**

❑ **What is your commitment toward how often to brainstorm with thumbnails?**

❑ **What seems like a doable weekly schedule that stretches you just a little?**

> "A poem is never finished; it's always an accident that puts a stop to it."
>
> —Paul Valéry

If you're having trouble coming up with a weekly schedule, consider starting with this sample schedule:

- ❑ **Monday: 25 minutes of creating, brain-drain writing, sketch out one thumbnail.**

- ❑ **Tuesday: 25 minutes of creating, brain-drain writing, intuitive painting.**

- ❑ **Wednesday: 25 minutes of creating, brain-drain writing, read about an artist you admire.**

- ❑ **Thursday: 25 minutes of creating, brain-drain writing, read about a technique you want to refine.**

- ❑ **Friday: 25 minutes of creating, brain-drain writing, call one of your accountability artists.**

PART 2: LIST YOUR TOP FIVE GOALS

Take out your journal and list your current top five art goals and aspirations for your art and art career. Consider the following:

- ❑ **Do you want to create a cohesive body of work?**

- ❑ **Do you want to work larger or smaller?**

- ❑ **Do you want to show in galleries?**

- ❑ **Do you want a large social media account?**

- ❑ **Would you love to be a full-time artist making a living entirely from your art?**

- ❑ **Do you want to be recognized as an artist in your community?**

- ❑ **Is there a class you would like to take?**

- ❑ **Or an art school you would love to attend?**

- ❑ **Do you want to appear in art magazines?**

- ❑ **Do you want to draw every day or paint once a week from a live model?**

PART 3: WRITE FIVE ACTION STEPS FOR EACH GOAL

Break down each of your top five goals into small, achievable action steps. Think about the smallest actions you can take. For example, if your goal is to gain gallery representation:

- ❑ **Research and create a list of ten galleries I truly have a chance of getting into.**
- ❑ **Update my website.**
- ❑ **Write my artist statement.**
- ❑ **Write or update my artist bio.**
- ❑ **Write a cover letter to each gallery.**

PART 4: A PLAN OF ACTION

Create a calendar where you plot out when you will take each action each month. Be realistic about your time commitments, and make sure your schedule works for you. This will help you stay organized and focused on the steps needed to achieve your goals. I like to put a little gold star on my weekly plan each day that I complete the tasks!

WHAT YOU WILL GAIN FROM THIS

This exercise will help you create a plan for ensuring your newfound habits become lasting ones. You'll create a plan that integrates the framework in this book of clearing blocks with brain-drain writing, creating a habit with 25 minutes a day, entering flow with intuitive painting, brainstorming with thumbnails and knowing your world with creative resources. By committing to this plan of action, you'll maintain the momentum that you've gained so far and continue to have breakthroughs and epiphanies. You'll also take time to consider your current artistic goals and the specific action steps that need to be taken to move forward on them.

"The only time I feel alive is when I'm painting."

–Vincent van Gogh

week

the list

12

It's time to make a final list of the artistic elements you want to incorporate in your work. The trick is that you want your artistic voice and style to be cohesive, without feeling like you're confined to a prison that you're trapped in for the rest of your life.

> *"Thinking in terms of a direction of curiosity and setting some parameters (which aren't too constraining but offer a flexible visual framework) allows for experimentation while also creating a cohesive body of work."*
>
> —Aleah Chapin

Now, with your connection to your authentic self-expression awakened, it's time to consciously chart your path forward. Even at this stage, you may be uncertain about which symbols and motifs to incorporate into your art. At the beginning of this course, you identified the components of your voice in Week 1 (page 20) and now, with the knowledge you've gained, you will make a new list of what excites and resonates with you. Your final list will serve as the foundation upon which your creative identity is built.

Crafting this list can be a challenge, especially if you've tried many different styles and subjects. You might find, like me, that you're drawn to seemingly opposing elements. For instance, I enjoy three-dimensionally rendered figures and also like the flatness of ornate patterns and designs. Finding a way to incorporate these somewhat oppositional elements was the key to creating something truly unique to me. The first time I tried to blend these seemingly opposing elements, the result was my painting *Map of the Universe*, which became one of the main paintings in my exhibition *Portals*.

Kristy Gordon
Map of the Universe

148

I recently had a student in an online art program I teach ask me how she could add more meaning to her work. I told her that I couldn't tell her exactly what to add, and that she would have to find meaning inside herself. She said that she didn't know why this was such a block for her, so I advised her to look back at her intuitive paintings and other works and make a list of recurring motifs and symbolism so that she would have a database to draw upon. This was successful because when we looked at her work overall, we found that there was a recurring sense of mystical light illuminating her work, so she realized that to elevate the work-in-progress, she could deepen the meaning by enhancing the numinous sense of transcendent light weaving through the painting.

By compiling your definitive list, you'll clarify your vision and direction. This list will remind you of the key elements of your style so that you'll have coherence and unity in your body of work. With your artistic compass in hand, you'll be poised to navigate endless possibilities of self-expression.

A lot of people ask me how to find their signature style, so it's worth taking a closer look at this idea of "art style." The visual language of an artist's voice is comprised of two key elements: style and concept. Style encompasses elements such as color palette, line, composition and type of mark-making. Whereas concept refers to the message or narrative in your art.

John K., the creator of *The Ren & Stimpy Show*, said, "A person's style is an amalgamation of their weaknesses as an artist." It's funny, but it's also actually pretty true. I would say that throughout all my artistic phases, that's been true in different ways. Early on, my lack of technical skills brought a certain style to my work, and now my immersion in an academic training rooted in classical realism is almost like my weakness. It's one that I tried to fight for a while, but when I finally accepted that I'm probably just going to be painting things realistically, I was able to set myself free to create the work I feel is truly me. It's best not to get too preoccupied with defining your style prematurely. Instead, focus on creating the best art that you can. Style naturally evolves over time. For instance, my work has naturally evolved from an attempt to paint these big political ideas and social commentary, such as my painting *Candyland*, to a quieter exploration of transcendence and the divine, such as in *The Great Mystery*.

"If I create with my heart almost all my intentions remain. If it is with the head—almost nothing."

—Marc Chagall

"Whether you succeed or not is irrelevant,
there is no such thing. Making your unknown
known is the important thing."

–Georgia O'Keeffe

Kristy Gordon
Candyland

Many accomplished artists note that personal style involves just creating a lot of work until it naturally happens. We need to determine how to interrogate our own artistic motivations, says artist Scott Maier, "because it's so easy to default to whatever other people are doing and think we should be doing that." We can trick ourselves into "thinking that's the voice of authenticity, when it's not." Scott also says, "It's a problem that's particularly challenging for creative individuals in that one of our superpowers is absorbing the environment—we take in everything." And then we process it in our art. We need to find ways of not losing this superpower while also being able to distinguish our own authentic inclinations.

Because our work is constantly evolving, a lot of artists find it helpful to work in series or bodies of work. Many artists find it useful to set some parameters around the series, such as certain colors to work with or a question to explore. These parameters can give a cohesion to a body of work while not being too constraining, leaving lots of room for freedom and exploration. My current work almost always includes pinks and blues and explores the magical, mysticism and the future for humanity. These guidelines are super open, allowing me room for complete artistic freedom but also reminding me what I enjoy in art so that I can create a cohesive body of work that I delight in.

Many accomplished artists like Aleah Chapin talk about how helpful it is to gather all the art that you like to look for threads. Aleah says to pay attention to what "colors are coming through; is it minimalist or very busy; what kinds of moods and emotions are coming through; is it realist or abstract; what are the threads?" And also: "Take a good, long, honest look at your own work and see if you're actually doing what you like." The discovery that many artists make is that they're not doing what pleases them artistically. If this happens to you, make a checklist of the elements you love that you're not doing, and make a checklist of elements to incorporate into your future work.

"To be an artist is to believe in life."

—Henry Moore

Kristy Gordon (top left)
The Great Mystery

Aleah Chapin (top right)
First Light

Scott Maier (bottom right)
Sunrise, Horsetooth

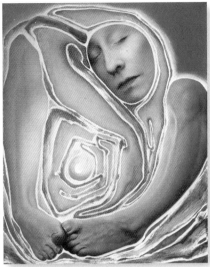

A paradox about developing our own unique artistic style is that focusing too much on creating a cohesive body of work can be an impairment. Artist John Sproul suggests we should try to explore and experiment with being as honest as possible with ourselves and not worry about creating a cohesive body of work initially. John found that "The honesty brings forward who you are, what you see and how you see into the work and that becomes the cohesiveness in the work."

Many artists are working within a multidisciplinary approach, exploring a particular theme in a variety of mediums. In this case, the work might look visually different from piece to piece, but there will be a unity in the concepts in the work. For instance, multidisciplinary artist Allison Green, who explores modes of femininity in her work, says, "A cohesive voice for me has meant a love of material itself. I develop a relationship with fabric, clay, drawing, assemblage and anything I see expressive potential in." In that way each work tells a related story such as in her fabric soft sculpture *Irons*, which continues her exploration of domesticity and her love of materials.

This week you'll consider your own motivations and fascinations to find what the defining aspects of your voice and your art style are. One of the best pieces of art advice I ever heard is, "Show me how you see the world." Often the way you see the world is so ingrained that it's almost invisible. That is why you will now revisit your original list from Week 1 (page 20), solidify what you've learned and reflect on your new insights about your artistic voice.

Kristy Gordon (top left)
In studio

John Sproul (bottom left)
Take My Order

Allison Green
(left of caption)
Irons

assignment

Now is the time to make *the list*. Having completed this program, take an inventory of the elements you want to incorporate in your work.

PART 1: THE LIST

Take out your notebook and make notes on the following:

❏   **The main themes or concepts you are drawn to**

❏   **Recurring symbolism or motifs**

❏   **Sizes or formats that speak to you**

❏   **Stylistic elements that you enjoy such as line quality, mark-making or edge quality**

❏   **Elements from your background that inform your work**

❏   **Your favorite colors or the color palette that you want to use**

❏   **The mood or feeling you want your work to convey**

You will be able to go back to this list whenever you are stuck or want to add something but don't quite know what.

PART 2: QUESTIONNAIRE FOR ARTISTS

Answer the following questions with your initial gut response. Then take time to revisit your answers and delve deeper into your thoughts and feelings. Look for epiphanies or surprising insights that may reveal your unique point of view:

❏   **When and where were you happiest creating?**

❏   **Who are your favorite artists?**

❏   **What is your all-time favorite work of art?**

❏   **What do you hate seeing in other artists' work?**

- [ ] What is your favorite artwork you've ever created?

- [ ] What are your favorite novels or movies?

- [ ] What are your favorite time periods in art history?

- [ ] What recurring themes and techniques do you see in your past work?

- [ ] What do you wish you'd see in galleries that you don't see—what's missing?

- [ ] What is your first memory of creating art and what were you creating?

- [ ] What is the first thing you think of in response to "How do you see the world?"

PART 3: REFLECTION

Once you've completed both parts of the assignment, take some time to reflect on insights you've gained about your artistic voice. How do your answers to the questionnaire and your comprehensive list intersect? What themes or patterns are emerging that define your unique perspective as an artist?

WHAT YOU WILL GAIN FROM THIS

Without this step you may continue to feel adrift. This list will act as your compass, guiding you as you navigate creative waters. This exercise will serve as a valuable resource as you continue to explore and develop a cohesive body of work.

Your artistic voice will continue to evolve, but you will find that the threads you have uncovered in this course will spark interest that will continue to fascinate you and show up in your work.

"The meaning of life is to find your gift.
The purpose of life is to give it away."

—Pablo Picasso

week

talking about
your art

13

Now that you've uncovered your artistic voice, you may wonder how to describe your work to another person. As artists, many of us have a deathly fear of talking about our art, and we often freeze when asked about it. This is where the Artist's Elevator Pitch comes in handy.

"An elevator pitch is essentially a very quick way for you to describe your work so that whoever's listening understands it and remembers it. At the core of who we are as humans is storytelling. We either love to gossip or tell stories, so that is essentially the reason behind elevator pitch."

—Marina Press Granger, founder of The Artist Advisory

Do you feel terrified when talking about your art? When someone asks what kind of work you create, do you answer in just a few words, closing the conversation as quickly as possible? Or do you find yourself talking forever, trapping the person in a long conversation as you struggle to explain your art? That's why having a prepared response is crucial. Not only does it prevent freezing, but it also clarifies your intentions so you can convey them in a concise and memorable way.

I used to have a little heart attack anytime anyone asked me about my work and quickly say, "I'm a representational figurative painter," putting an abrupt end to the conversation. I had no idea how to describe my art, and I felt so much pressure as soon as the question was posed.

That's why Marina Press Granger, the founder of The Artist Advisory, proposes a three-part formula for the artist's elevator pitch:

❑ **Why you do what you do**

❑ **How your perspective informs your work**

❑ **What you actually do (explain what your work looks like)**

Let's look at the three components in a little more detail.

The first part is where we explain why we create the work we do. Marina explains, "At the core of everything we do is our intention—the why." So we start by describing the themes or ideas that interest us and inform our decisions as we create our art. I neglected this component in my elevator pitch for a very long time, and it turned out to be the missing link.

The second element is how our background informs our work, and this is often the vulnerable piece that a lot of people don't want to share because it is too personal. However, Marina points out that "When you go to a museum and read the wall tags, you will know why every artist did what they did and how their perspective informs their work, because that's what puts it into context." She further explains, "When the artwork is in context, it goes to the museum level." Our background can include our history, socioeconomic status, past occupations or anything that informs our perspective as an artist. This context is the common denominator in all your work. As vulnerable as this component can be, it is what hooks people's attention and makes our pitch memorable.

Finally, we describe what our work actually looks like. We find a way to describe it so that if it isn't in front of a person, they will get a visual image.

Author Sam Horn suggests delaying this revelation of your work. He says, "Next time someone asks you what you do, don't tell them." He advises keeping the conversation open for as long as possible and to delay telling them what you actually do, which is exactly what we're doing with this format for the artist's elevator pitch.

So now, instead of saying "I'm a figurative artist," I say, "I've always seen the world with a sense of magic (the why). Growing up, my mom told me about mystical experiences she'd had, and that when my granddad was passing over, he got glimpses into another world where he could see people talking about him, so he knew when he was going to die (my perspective/ background). So I paint strange and surreal interactions between humans, animals and hybrid creatures that explore magic, mystery and the future for humanity (what I do)."

Can you see how much more engaging this is and how you get a sense of the backstory behind my work? There is usually a piece in our pitch that feels very vulnerable to share. It's the part we think maybe we can leave out. For me, I really didn't want to tell people about my mom's mystical experiences or my granddad's glimpses into another realm. These experiences felt way too personal, yet they are the foundation of my perspective and the way I see the world with a sense of magic.

Kristy Gordon
Portals **installation at The Gallery at Greenly Center**

In working with artists in an online art program I teach, I discovered that almost every artist wants to find a way around sharing the aspects of their personal history that inform their work. The artist Tun Myaing points out, "Although we get so self-conscious explaining our work in a personal way, as the listener, they just take it at face value since they have no other frame of reference for you." And that is the exact part that hooks the listener, engages their interest and makes them feel a connection to the work and the artist.

Regardless of our background, when we hit on that personal piece, it always feels very intimate. This may prompt an instinct to conceal it, although as the listener, it often doesn't sound like a big deal. While your vulnerable element may seem inconsequential enough to leave out, it often resonates powerfully with your audience. Embrace it, as it distinguishes your work from mere trend following.

Kristy Gordon (above)
Ripple in Reality

Kristy Gordon (right)
Map of the Universe

"Art washes away
from the soul the dust
of everyday life."

–Pablo Picasso

To this day, I still freeze up a bit whenever someone poses the dreaded question "What kind of work do you do?" Yet I've found that as I say my first few memorized, simple words—"I've always seen the world with a sense of magic . . ."—the rest starts to flow out of me. The first few words are like a lubricant that eases the conversation.

Tun noticed that at different functions and depending on whom you're talking to, you might tweak what you say a bit. For example, if you're talking to an art director about your work, you might want to emphasize how your work fits into the context of what they show at the gallery. This can be useful, for example, in what you write in a cover letter for a submission to a gallery. Whereas when you meet a doctor or a lawyer at an art show, if you use any "art talk," it will exclude them, and they may feel like they don't understand art; therefore talking about your personal experience and backstory is a much better way to help them engage with your work.

It's important not to say absolutely everything you can think of all at once, potentially trapping the person and making them regret asking. Start with those three concise sentences, and it will organically open a deeper conversation if the person desires that.

Once you've honed your elevator pitch and gained clarity about your intention, you can tie that into everything you do—the way you present your work will be affected, as will the galleries or venues you choose to exhibit in and even your approach to social media. For instance, on social media, you can include your intention in the captions of your posts and also share posts from other accounts that are related to your perspective in your stories. Marina points out that you can include a segment of your elevator pitch in the tagline of your bio on social media to give everyone a lens through which they can look at your work. Keep your intention in mind at all times, and it will even help clarify your direction for future work.

Tun Myaing
The Metal Dome in the Boiler Room

assignment

Your assignment this week is to develop your Artist's Elevator Pitch. A significant challenge arises as many of us explore multiple subject matters and various types of work, especially early on in our artistic journeys. That's why identifying the themes underlying our work is useful, as it establishes common ground across our diverse artistic creations. Delving into how our background shapes our artistic perspective first, and reserving an actual description of our work until the end, proves to be an engaging and memorable way to discuss our art.

Here is the basic format that Marina Press Granger suggests:

❑   **Why you do what you do.**

❑   **How your perspective informs your work.**

❑   **What you actually do (explain what your work looks like).**

To discover your perspective, ask yourself:

❑   **How would you describe your art—what does it look like?**

❑   **What subject matter do you explore and what are the themes?**

❑   **When is the first time you became interested in these subjects?**

❑   **Where do you live or where do you create your work?**

❑   **Is there anything from your background, your childhood, your life experience or a past career that informs your perspective?**

❑   **Is there a contrast between what you create and what you experienced in the past?**

❑   **When did you start to create art or when did you decide to become an artist?**

"I am seeking. I am striving. I am in it with all my heart."

—Vincent van Gogh

As you develop your pitch remember:

- ❑ Don't start with "When I was growing up . . ." It's too cliché. Instead begin by mentioning what interests you.

- ❑ Initially keep your elevator pitch to three sentences. This will open a conversation if the viewer wants to talk more.

- ❑ Resist the urge to leave out the vulnerable parts. These personal elements from your background are what will help people connect with you and your work.

- ❑ Formulate your Artist's Elevator Pitch into a few sentences that take less than 1 minute to say, and practice it every day in front of the mirror this week.

WHAT YOU WILL GAIN FROM THIS

This exercise will help you explain your work in an engaging way to another person. Once you have your elevator pitch, you can tie this into the ways you present your work. (For instance, what you write in the captions or stories of posts on social media.) This will also help you clarify your own perspective so you understand your intentions even more deeply, which can guide the development of your future work.

"Every good painter paints what he is."

—Jackson Pollock

"I never paint dreams or nightmares. I paint my own reality."

—Frida Kahlo

epilogue

"The thing that surprises artists the most is when suddenly something shows up in your studio and you don't know what to make of it. It can be a little frightening to let go of what you may think of yourself or what other people may think of you and to strike off in a new direction."

—Peter Drake

It's important to be aware that even once we've found our artistic voice, it will continue to evolve.

In order to keep our artistic practice vital and authentic, we must allow our work to shift and change as we grow and transform as human beings.

I can relate to this evolution in my own life. In my early twenties, I started having some success as a landscape painter, and it was exhilarating to see my paintings selling well. I painted every day and felt like my life was complete. But then something happened. I started to be called in a different direction—I believe it was the calling of my soul. I suddenly felt uninspired, as if I were just a glorified photocopy machine. This was the same feeling that had caused me to leave my animation job to become a full-time artist. I suddenly felt like I would have been better off staying in animation; it was definitely better money.

My worst fear then came true. I felt like I never wanted to paint again. I completed the paintings for a solo show that was approaching and then never ever painted that type of work again. I allowed myself to move in a different direction.

There can be pressure from the art market or a certain clientele to just stick with that same thing for the rest of your life once you've developed a name for yourself. Some artists sacrifice themselves and do exactly that, but the greatest artists bravely allow their work to evolve, even if it means leaving some of their following behind.

Neil Gaiman once said, "Whether or not people love the next thing you do does not matter. Audiences, fans, only ever want one thing, which is more of what they liked last time, and it is your job as an artist not to give that to them. What you have to give them is what they don't know they want."

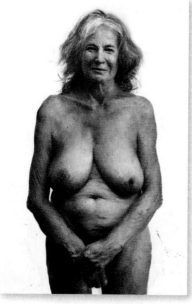

Kristy Gordon (top)
Transmutation

Aleah Chapin (bottom)
Auntie

In her journey to find her artistic voice, Aleah Chapin made the conscious decision to put aside what anyone else thought and paint only what she truly wanted. This decision led her to create her painting *Auntie*, which won the BP Portrait Award in 2012, and skyrocketed her to art fame. Aleah says everything about *Auntie* felt vulnerable, from doing a nude photoshoot with her relatives to creating such a personal painting of her family, but she was following her commitment to paint what truly interested her. This same commitment continues to infuse vitality in her artistic practice today, giving her the courage to allow her voice to evolve despite pressure to create work just like her award-winning work.

Freedom isn't given; freedom is taken. We must give ourselves permission— nobody else can. Even though Aleah's work was appearing in magazines and selling out at shows globally, she followed her inner impulses, and her new work feels even more genuine and true to her than ever before.

In an interview I conducted with Peter Drake on my podcast *Down2Art*, he emphasized that as we evolve, we should explore new techniques, research methods and perhaps embrace new technologies in our work. Making art is about remaining open, and while it can be tempting to create what pleases others, for our practice to retain vitality, we must allow it to change.

Peter points out that some artists find a signature style and do that for the rest of their lives. This is a very business-oriented approach to art, but a lot of people think this is how to survive in the art world. As tempting as it may be to create what pleases others, Peter says, "That's the deadliest approach to a studio practice. It's so self-limiting, and it's really more about business."

Steven Assael warns that as artists age, there's a risk of just repeating themselves and becoming like a parody of themselves. To avoid this, we need to keep pushing new grounds to maintain the same vitality that initially drove us.

Steven Assael (top)
Passengers

Peter Drake (bottom)
Drake in studio with *Riders*

Also, remember you're always just one artwork away from an expression that truly feels true to you, but don't put that pressure on every work you make. As Elizabeth Gilbert says about writing, approach each work as though it was the most important thing you've ever done while being ready to delete it entirely if needed. The more you can convince yourself that it's not that important, the more freedom you'll find in your artistic expression.

Neil Gaiman wrote, "If you're doing it right, you should feel while you're doing it that you're revealing a little too much of yourself." Embrace imperfection because as Neil puts it, "The only thing that is perfect is a blank piece of paper, untouched with nothing on it."

As you go forth on your journey, remember the most important advice I have ever received. My hippie friend, placing his hand on my heart, said, "Don't draw back from anything you feel is important." Those words became the guiding principle of my life. Let these words guide you whenever you have an impulse to try something in your art.

"You come to nature with all her theories, and she knocks them all flat."
—Pierre Auguste Renoir

"There's no retirement for an artist, it's your way of living so there's no end to it."
—Henry Moore

acknowledgments

I am profoundly grateful to the great spirit of inspiration that moved through me, guiding me throughout the journey of writing this book. Looking back, I can see how many years of my life were perfectly orchestrated, leading me to the precise knowledge and insights I would need to craft this book. I'm grateful to my amazing editor, Franny Donington, who magically found me and reached out—leading to a book deal that seemed to simply fall in my lap. I extend my heartfelt appreciation to Franny and William Kiester, the publisher, for being so open to my ideas and their willingness to let me follow my heart and explore my own voice.

I also want to express my gratitude to Liz Adams for her dedicated reading of numerous chapters and her insightful feedback. My heartfelt thanks go to Liz and Manu Saluja for their weekly calls that have kept me on track for so many years. I'm also indebted to Kayla Yoder, whose meticulous editing of the sample chapter transformed it into a compelling piece.

Additionally, I want to acknowledge the support and inspiration provided by Patricia Watwood and Daniel Maidman, both talented artists who had ventured into the realm of writing. Their encouragement and belief in my writing capabilities convinced me that I, too, could undertake this remarkable journey.

Thank you all so much for your immense contributions to this book!

about the author

Kristy Gordon has exhibited her work in solo and group exhibitions throughout Canada, the United States, Europe and China at venues including the European Museum of Modern Art in Barcelona, Spain, and the National Academy Museum in New York City. She is an adjunct professor at New York Academy of Art. Kristy received a BFA from Ontario College of Art and Design in 2011 and an MFA from New York Academy of Art in 2013. As a three-time recipient of the Elizabeth Greenshields Foundation Grant, her work has won numerous awards and honors. Kristy's work and art writing have been featured in various publications, including *The Artist's Magazine*, *International Artist* and *Fine Art Connoisseur*. Kristy's paintings hang in more than 600 collections worldwide, including the Government of Ontario Art Collection. At the time of writing this, Kristy is represented by Grenning Gallery in Sag Harbor, New York; Garvey|Simon in New York City; and Studio Sixty Six in Ottawa, Canada. Visit her website at kristygordon.com or follow her on Instagram @kristygordonart.

contributing artists

Bev Gordon, *Sentinel*, page 10

Jessica Gordon, *Ontario Forest*, page 10

Philip Craig, *Lily Pads on a Pond During Sunrise*, page 11

Shannon Craig, *Approaching Rain*, page 11

Juan Martínez, *Hummingbirds*, page 13

Gaetanne Lavoie, *The Double Plus One*, page 16

Enrique Martínez Celaya, from left, page 23: *The Same Places*, *The Words*

Jason Yarmosky, *Sleep Walking*, page 23

Hieronymus Bosch, *The Garden of Earthly Delights*, page 24–25

Jan van Eyck, *The Crucifixion; The Last Judgment*, page 26

Carolyn Janssen, *~*(G.O.E.D.)*~*, page 27

John O'Connor, *Conspiracy: Faker Sent INN*, page 37

Daniel Maidman, *Natasha*, page 40

Katherine Bradford, *Storm at Sea*, page 47

Brian Cirmo, *Bulb*, page 51

Lisa Lebofsky, *Ilulissat Glacier*, page 61

Kelsey Tynik, *Sometimes human places, create inhuman monsters*, page 61

Sherlin Hendrick, *Anxiety Rabbit*, page 61

The Artist's Magazine, September 2015 cover, page 72

Manu Saluja, *Wisdom*, page 73

Michelle Doll, *Family Portrait (Miller-Vargas)*, page 74

Buket Savci, *Suspended in a Sunbeam*, page 75

Jeremy Lipking, *Riders Under Vermilion Cliffs*, page 80

Casey Baugh, *Game of Love*, page 85

Steven Assael, *D*, page 86

Ailyn Lee, *Break a Leg*, page 88

Ailyn Lee, idea sketch of *Break a Leg*, page 88

Sherlin Hendrick, *Jackal & Hide*, page 89

Sherlin Hendrick, *Jackal & Hide* maquette, page 89

Jacob Hicks, *Woman 46, God of Small Things*, page 95

Peter Drake, *McBroke*, page 96

Kyle Staver, *Dusk*, page 98

Kyle Staver, *Dawn*, page 99

Noelle Timmons, *Jacki's House*, page 105

Lily Koto Olive, *Until Healing Begins*, page 105

Manu Saluja, *The Unraveling*, page 107

Liz Adams, *Religieuse aux Framboises*, page 107

Aleah Chapin, *It Was the Sound of Their Feet*, page 108

Alonsa Guevara, *Ghaf & Migration: Observing the Unknown*, page 110

Patricia Watwood, *Femen Flora*, page 118

Naruki Kukita, *The Death of Virtual Marat*, page 119

Alicia Brown, *Citizen in the Promise Land*, page 120–121

Amy Bennett, *Flirt*, page 122

Amy Bennett, model for *Packages*, page 122

Ron Lambert, *Ossify*, page 123

Ron Lambert, *Ossify* maquette, page 123

Michela Martello, *Prophecy Garden*, page 130

Rembrandt van Rijn, *The Toilet of Bathsheba*, page 132

Julia Jenkins, *Solar Sorceress*, page 133

Julia Jenkins, *The Alchemist*, page 134

Dina Brodsky, *Sketchbook*, page 141

Aleah Chapin, *First Light*, page 153

Scott Maier, *Sunrise, Horsetooth*, page 153

John Sproul, *Take My Order*, page 154

Allison Green, *Irons*, page 155

Tun Myaing, *The Metal Dome in the Boiler Room*, page 164

Aleah Chapin, *Auntie*, page 168

Steven Assael, *Passengers*, page 169

Peter Drake, Drake in studio with *Riders*, page 169

index